IGNITE
YOUR LIFE

Barry Meguiar is the greatest personal soul winner I know. His love for God is reflected by how he lives his life and shares his faith. In this powerful book, Barry instructs, inspires, and encourages us to walk confidently in the divine purpose we all share: moving everyone, every day, closer to Jesus. I believe this is one of the most important books you'll read this year. Be prepared to have your faith strengthened and your life changed!

—TOMMY BARNETT
COPASTOR, DREAM CITY CHURCH, PHOENIX;
LOS ANGELES DREAM CENTER

From the first time I met Barry Meguiar, I knew he was a man on whom the Lord had laid His hand in a significant way. As I observed him, I witnessed that Barry was driven with a deep commitment to win men and women to Jesus Christ. Barry has been an outstanding businessman, having led Meguiar's Car Wax to be a premiere company. However, the real passion that drives Barry is three-fold. One is his dedication and love for Jesus Christ. Second is the desire to introduce men and women to a life-changing experience as followers of Jesus Christ. Third is that Barry has an infectious spirit that draws people to him and his dear wife, Karen. One will discover, after reading this book, that to live a life committed to Jesus Christ is a life of great joy and most rewarding. As the title of the book states, *Ignite Your Life* is Barry's desire for others!

—DR. THOMAS TRASK
FORMER GENERAL SUPERINTENDENT, ASSEMBLIES OF GOD

When I grow up, I want to be like Barry Meguiar. Why? He is the consummate joyful Christian, and as we all know the joy of the Lord really is our strength. Secondly, when I see the culture as "hostile," Barry views it as open to the gospel. When I see some people beyond reach, Barry views them as people wanting Jesus. I am ashamed to say there are days in which I am like the shoe salesman a century ago who was sent to a primitive tribe and wrote back, "Get me out of here. No one here wears shoes." In contrast, Barry is like the salesman a century ago who was sent to a primitive tribe who wrote back, "Send me all the shoes you have. No one here has any."

—JIM GARLOW
COFOUNDER, WELL VERSED

What a privilege it is to know Barry Meguiar. It wasn't until a few years after our friendship started that I realized he was best friends with David Wilkerson for decades and would sit as friends with David Wilkerson and Leonard Ravenhill. If you're wondering where the spiritual passion comes from, it in part comes from rubbing shoulders with these spiritual giants. Barry is kind, generous, a soul winner, and kingdom minded. He has truly expended his life in service of God and others. Many know him as an extraordinarily successful businessman, but he is really a powerful servant in God's kingdom. I couldn't be more excited about this book because Barry is constantly igniting others with a spiritual passion. His story will inspire you and change your life.

—MATT BROWN
EVANGELIST; AUTHOR, *TRUTH PLUS LOVE*;
FOUNDER, THINK ETERNITY

I just finished reading *Ignite Your Life*, and it was a fantastic inspiration to my life! Thank you, Barry Meguiar, for producing this powerful masterpiece with scriptural and personal experience to encourage and equip Christians everywhere to be about the Lord's business moving everyone, every day, closer to Jesus. I highly recommend this book, especially for these times in which we live. It's engaging, entertaining, scriptural, challenging, inspiring, and life changing. I plan to use this book in our next Bott Radio Network staff meeting. Let's get off the bench!

—RICH BOTT
PRESIDENT AND CEO, BOTT RADIO NETWORK

Barry has been a personal friend for decades. He is passionate about evangelism and walks his talk. He is eager to share his faith in a sensitive and loving way with everyone the Lord puts him in contact with. His life is extremely exemplary—and it follows that he would write a book about how we can be the same way as it relates to turning the world upside down by sharing our faith with others in a more deliberate and outward manner. Barry, rightly so, puts to bed the false adage that the best way to witness is by not speaking words.

—Ralph Drollinger
President and Founder, Capitol Ministries

Barry Meguiar has an infectious love of Jesus Christ, and it shines through in this important book. If you want to live the victorious Christian life and share the joy, peace, and contentment that come from selling out to Jesus, then *Ignite Your Life* is for you.

—Floyd Brown
Founder, The Western Journal

Barry Meguiar is a car guy with an incredible exuberance for the Lord and life. If your spiritual engine is idling, read this book and get it supercharged. Barry shows you how to get passion back in your life while making your witness to others a great joy. In these troubled times, the fields are white for harvest. *Ignite Your Life* offers you a way to supercharge your spiritual engine through the "sport" of sharing your faith. It changed the way I look at my responsibility to serve the Lord Jesus Christ. *Ignite Your Life* will encourage you to serve through what can only be described as a breakthrough in sharing your faith. It's fun, it's easy, and it takes the fear out of speaking up for Jesus. Best of all, it will renew your joy as you watch the Lord use you for His kingdom. It's time to ignite your engine!

—Ken Eldred
Entrepreneur; Cofounder/CEO, Living Stones
Foundation; Author, *The Integrated Life*

Barry has not only written an influential book, he lives an influential life. This is a call to awaken the power of love that

God has vested in all of us. Barry and my late father, David Wilkerson, were best friends, kingdom co-laborers, and men cut from the same cloth. Like my dad, Barry deeply loves God and those Jesus gave His life for on the cross. The tide of spiritual and moral decline in our nation will not be remedied by politics, religion, media, academia, or Wall Street. Our nation's only hope is simply found in people who are living, showing, and sharing the love of God to others. The world is hungry for the love of God. I'm wholeheartedly endorsing this book because I believe it will help us become likeminded people in the sharing of God's love, and the world will be changed.

—GARY WILKERSON
PRESIDENT, WORLD CHALLENGE

My friend Barry Meguiar has written a book from his life experiences. Encompassing each one is his steadfast faith in God and His promises. From those who know Barry personally to those who recognize his product line in the automotive world, what is more famous than the Meguiar name is the spirit behind this man. Rooted in God, Barry's life has been beyond what anyone could ask—a man whom God has not only used but clearly given a plan and path to fulfill. This is a man whom I have seen personally walk with Jesus through highs and lows, from the celebration of life to mourning the loss of a child.

Barry has put together an exceptional book that I encourage everyone to read. A quick browse of the chapter titles will show you that they can stand alone and serve as a devotion to something you may be going through at any given time. God has blessed Barry, and he continues to be a blessing. He and his wife, Karen, are treasures in the kingdom of God. I highly recommend this book—keep it close and make it a reference often in your time of devotion with God.

—JACK HIBBS
SENIOR AND FOUNDING PASTOR, CALVARY CHAPEL
CHINO HILLS

IGNITE
YOUR LIFE

BARRY
MEGUIAR

CHARISMA
HOUSE

Visit the author's website at https://igniteamerica.com.

Cataloging-in-Publication Data is on file with the Library of Congress.
International Standard Book Number: 978-1-63641-151-4
E-book ISBN: 978-1-63641-153-8

While the author has made every effort to provide accurate internet addresses at the time of publication, neither the publisher nor the author assumes any responsibility for errors or for changes that occur after publication. Further, the publisher does not have any control over and does not assume any responsibility for author or third-party websites or their content.

4 2024
Printed in the United States of America

*This book is dedicated to my incredible parents,
who taught me the ways of the Lord when
I was young, always encouraged me, never
shied away from disciplining me, and role-
modeled for me how I should live my life.*

MALCOLM AND MABEL MEGUIAR

*I can't wait to see them again and
thank them for eternity.*

CONTENTS

ACKNOWLEDGMENTS

IT WOULD DISHONOR God if I did not acknowledge those He placed in my life to put up with me, correct me, inspire me, and love me in spite of me. I'm an amalgamation of their collective devotion to God and love for His Word, and their ability to speak truth into my life.

First and foremost, I want to honor my wife, Karen, who has not only been beside me all of our married years but often running ahead of me. She's amazing! Then we've had our two extraordinary daughters, Michelle and Nicole, who have mentored me all their lives. We lost our mega soul winner, Nicole, three years ago, and Michelle is working on her master's degree in theology while being a chaplain at Sharp Memorial Hospital in San Diego. Michelle's husband, Scott Shoemaker, is head of Admissions at Point Loma Nazarene University, also in San Diego.

We have the six greatest grandkids, all in college or graduated, starting with our lead dog, Ryan Shoemaker, his amazing brother, Jason Shoemaker, and my favorite granddaughter, Alex Shoemaker. Then we have three grandsons from Nicole, with the oldest being AJ, followed by Jordan and Elijah, who have all survived the loss of their mom and are making her and the Lord proud.

Then there's Mike and Leslie Kennedy, our "non-family member" family members, who have been with me for over forty years, guiding and directing and making our collective dreams become reality as business colleagues at Meguiar's and ministry partners at Ignite America, along with Katie Pender, who runs all of our social media platforms.

Dr. Doug Petersen has been my irreplaceable friend, mentor, and ministry partner for over fifty years. This precious evangelist, pastor, missionary, ministry leader, professor, and world-class theologian, having received his doctorate from Oxford, has always been my go-to guy for keeping me theologically correct.

My newest friend and now brother, Max Davis, was introduced

to me by Charisma Media. This precious man of God, filled and empowered by the Holy Spirit, guided me through this book writing experience with love, patience, and wisdom—encouraging, correcting, and inspiring me at all the right times to get everything I wanted to say said.

Of course, the irreplaceable gifts for every Christ follower are those who are always there praying for you and on-the-ready to help you at any moment. The joy of the Lord is my strength—along with the unending love and support I treasure from my Christ-following friends.

INTRODUCTION

I HOPE YOU'LL ENJOY reading this book as much as I enjoyed writing it. I'm free from the protocols of being an academic or a pastor because, like most of you, I'm a layman. And I'll always be indebted to the generations of dedicated Christians, on both sides of my family, who passed their legacy down to me.

If I have a unique point of view, it comes from seeking God all my life, challenging the Scriptures, proving the Scriptures, and then applying the Scriptures to my life—all while building Meguiar's Car Wax from a small family business into a global brand. It was about halfway through my journey that I discovered how easy it is to replace fear with unwavering, wholehearted faith. That's when I began living in the sweet spot with God, knowing He was directing my steps.

No matter the color of our skin or our political persuasion, all of us know our world is out of control, and it's way bigger than politics. Whether or not we choose to admit it, we know there's no person or organization with enough power to create this level of chaos all over the world at the same time. That's the real reason most Americans are living in fear. It's only by looking through the lens of Scripture that we can fully understand who's causing the chaos and how we can stop him.

Deep down, all of us know the further we get away from God, the more we'll experience turmoil. And the closer we get to God, the more we'll find ourselves bonded together with peace and joy and love. You can't change the world. But you can change *your* world. And when all of us change *our* worlds, we'll change the world. It's up to us!

This is a book of scriptures that will ignite your life—when you put them in context and start living them. At the end of each chapter you'll find the scriptures you encountered in that chapter listed so you have them all in one place for studying in a small group or on your own. My heart's desire is to show you how I discovered these biblical truths and how their practical applications have ignited my life forever—and will ignite yours as well.

If you want to conquer worry and doubt, you're going to love this book!

ONE MORE THING...

In several places throughout this book you will find QR codes. These are mobile bar codes embedded with content that smartphone users can access. Each code will instantly direct you to bonus videos that will further explore the concepts we will be discussing.

IGNITE YOUR LIFE

If you do not have a smartphone, don't worry. Simply visit https://igniteamerica.com/iylbook/ and click on the various links to access the same bonus material.

CHAPTER 1

THE STARTING LINE

THIS BOOK IS about igniting your life no matter where you are right now. Rich or poor, Christian or non-Christian, God loves us all the same—as much as He's ever loved anyone. And His primary desire for you is that you spend eternity with Him.

We've made it so difficult when it's so easy and so much fun to live our lives God's way. The wealth of scriptures within these pages will change your life if you'll take the time to read them. Far beyond my personal experiences and what you've been taught in church about evangelism, this is a presentation of God's Word speaking directly to the fiber of your life and setting you free. John 8:32 tells us: "Then you will know the truth, and the truth will set you free."

I love every part of my life, from my business and being a "car guy" who enjoys cool cars, to being a beach bum and a sports nut, loving great places and great meals, having the best friends on the planet, and most importantly, being blessed with my amazing wife and family. God wants us to enjoy everything He places in our lives, as long as He remains our first love. Second Corinthians 4:18 reminds us: "For the things which are seen are temporal, but the things which are not seen are eternal" (KJV).

Yes, I'm a car guy to the bone, and I love creating perfect paint finishes on great cars. But it's honoring God that pushed me to do that to the very limits of my ability. That driving force inside of me has defined a large portion of my life and satisfaction.

Few people have the perspective of car guys and the car hobby like I have. We sponsor and experience all types of car shows all over the world, and I can tell you that car guys (ladies who love cars are "car guys" too) are among the best people on earth. When speaking to car guy groups, I often say, "If you could earn your way to heaven, car guys would be at the front of the line!" But getting into heaven has nothing to do with what we do and everything to do with what Jesus did for us on the cross.

And that brings us to the starting line of eternity. Yes, I love living life to the fullest, enjoying every moment of it. But I know it's all going away soon, and very soon, and that's why I love the song "This World Is Not My Home" by Jim Reeves. A hundred years from now the only thing that will matter is how many people will be in heaven because of your influence. There is no higher calling in your life!

Our life on earth is merely an internship for heaven. God has given us a limited number of years to (1) learn who Jesus is and what He did for us, (2) make our decision to accept Jesus Christ as our Savior and Lord, and (3) help as many people as possible spend eternity with us in heaven.

Life is short and eternity is forever. The Bible says that our time on earth is "a vapor that appears for a little time and then vanishes away" (Jas. 4:14, NKJV). I know when I get to heaven, it's not going to matter how many bottles of car wax I sold. "It is appointed unto men once to die, but after this the judgment" (Heb. 9:27, KJV).

Your entrance into heaven will be wholly dependent on one deciding factor: Did you or did you not accept Jesus Christ as your Savior from hell and make Him the Lord of your life? Being a good person and doing good things with good intentions to honor God has nothing to do with your entrance into heaven. It comes down to this: Did you serve God or man with your life?

For those of us who accepted Jesus Christ as our Savior and are allowed into heaven, we'll receive eternal rewards based on how we used our "vapor" of time on earth to lead people to Jesus. "And then he will repay each person according to what he has done" (Matt. 16:27, ESV). That alone tells you that your most important task on earth is to lead people to Jesus.

Life is about redemption—pure and simple! As wonderful or as horrible as our lives might be at this moment, God wants to ignite our lives for His glory. No matter where you are with your life, God never leaves you nor forsakes you (Heb. 13:5), and He'll direct your steps (Ps. 37:23) when you trust Him with your whole heart and live for His purpose (Rom. 8:28). You see, there's no separation between living your life for God's purpose and God making everything in your life work for good as you enjoy unwavering (worry-free) faith. It's all connected. You're going to hear that a thousand times in this book; it's that important!

LIFE IS ABOUT REDEMPTION

Of course, it's possible to get to heaven without sharing your faith. Here's the problem: when you wholly accept Jesus Christ as your Savior and Lord, God becomes your first love (Rev. 2:1–7), and living for His purpose—known as doing the first work (v. 5)—becomes the driving force of your life. There's no escaping this connection. Sharing your faith is the barometer for where you are in your relationship with God. Case in point: you can't stop an exuberant new Christian from sharing their faith. That's how God expects you to live your entire life!

Here's the starting line for your walk with God: understand that everything you say and do is moving everyone watching you closer or further away from God. This ignites your life because it completely replaces your obligation to do the right things with *wanting* to do everything you can to lead people to Jesus. That's when there's purpose, eternal purpose, igniting you to honor God in everything you do.

Jesus was emphasizing this point when He said loving Him and loving our neighbors as ourselves fulfills all the commandments. You see, when you love your neighbors (everyone) as yourself, you're as concerned for their salvation as you are your own. At that point you'll do everything possible to lead everyone around you to Jesus, and you'll automatically fulfill the other eight commandments.

SURVIVING THE DAYS AHEAD

For your own spiritual health, you need to be moving everyone, every day, closer to Jesus and spending your quality time with friends who are doing it as well. The dedicated body of Christ is going to be of paramount importance as we face the challenges of living in the last days. I'll speak more to that later. But it's inconceivable how lukewarm Christians, who already live in fear today, will survive when the persecution of Christians becomes commonplace in America.

"This little light of mine, I'm going to let it shine" is more than a cute chorus. As a Christian, your light is growing brighter and needed more as our world gets darker. But you can choose to not let your light shine, to not let people know that you're a Christian (Matt. 5:15) by putting it under a bushel basket. That's exactly what most Christians are doing today. It's by our silence that we've allowed darkness to overtake America.

Most Christians feel good about the good they're doing, never thinking about the salvation of those around them. In fact, most Evangelicals believe being good is the same as sharing their faith. But being good and doing good things doesn't get you or anyone else into heaven.

A solid Christian friend of mine was proud to tell me how he had tipped a cleaning worker in a public restroom. It never occurred to my friend that he could have told that man God prompted him to give him that tip to let him know that God loves him. He was focused on the good he was doing rather than on the ministry he could have been doing. It takes the same amount of time! It just needs to be intentional. Most Christians make this mistake all day long. If Christians just started giving God the glory for the good they are doing, we'd ignite America with revival.

As I look back on my lifelong walk with God from the viewpoint of an eighty-year-old, I often say in jest, "Wow! The Scriptures actually work! Who knew?" I grew up attending church Sunday mornings, Sunday nights, Wednesday nights, and usually added special nights every week. I've heard thousands of sermons, and I'm still learning.

Here's my experience: the biblical teachings that have been preached, taught, and modeled for me, including my own lifelong deep dive into the Scriptures, have all proven themselves to be true. This includes one of the most profound Scripture verses of all: "Unless you change and become like little children, you will never enter the kingdom of heaven" (Matt. 18:3).

Nothing amazes me more than the truth of scriptures we've known from birth, quote without thinking, and yet routinely fail to do without giving it a second thought. And we miss the blessings that come from doing them, such as God protecting us, directing our steps, and making everything in our lives work for good. Then we blame God for not being there for us.

It bears repeating. God makes everything in our lives work for good when we love Him and live for His purpose (Rom. 8:28), to seek and save the lost, to move everyone, every day, closer to Jesus. This may be the most important verse in the Bible, after John 3:16.

God is promising, from now until you get to heaven, that He will make everything in your life work for good if you do these two things. But how many of us are loving God as our first love and living for His purpose, which is to seek and save the lost? I can't ask this question often enough. Why are we not hearing this message preached from our pulpits?

This is not an academic message for me. I've been to hell and back and found that God is even more real and His joy more full because of the bad times. There's no hope without God. In my worst moments, God has proven Himself to be faithful and His Word to be truth. He's taught us that we can always trust Him to make our paths straight and everything work for good. It's so simple! All we have to do is love Him and live our lives for His purpose. That's when our faith becomes effortless.

Spiritual growth spurts normally occur when we're in desperate need of His help. That's been particularly true in my life. Karen and I have watched God use the bad stuff in our lives for good so many times that now we get excited when things go wrong. After so many trials and miracles, we no longer get upset about anything. God is always there to accomplish His purpose. When you're living for God's purpose, there are no accidents or coincidences. It's actually an adventure when things go wrong. We've moved from asking for solutions to thanking Him in advance for the solutions!

Karen and I travel together everywhere. We have our routines down to including who sits next to the window on the plane. But on one flight we found that we were separated, sitting in two different rows. It was a surprise we didn't expect, but we always accept surprises as God being on the move. Nothing happens unless He allows it or ordains it. In my case, I found myself sitting next to a young girl who was charming. After we took off, I pulled out my Bible to let her know that I was a Christian, and she asked if I was a pastor. I said no, I'm just a businessman who loves God, and then I immediately changed the subject. I'm never pushy.

But I knew this was a divine appointment, and the Holy Spirit let her know she could trust me. It's amazing how quickly the Holy Spirit can touch an unbeliever's heart during these experiences. In fact, there's no question God had been working on her in advance, preparing her for our conversation. Within fifteen minutes she told me that God could never love her because she was in a relationship with another girl. Of course, I immediately explained how much God loved her and how there was nothing we can do to separate ourselves from God's love. It's not my job to judge or condemn anyone.

Our job is to love people into a relationship with Jesus Christ. At first she couldn't believe it, but the transformation of her life during that flight was amazing, and the smile and look of relief on her face showed it. She wasn't ready to accept the Lord yet, but she was very close, and we prayed together as the plane was landing. It was not an accident when Karen and I got separated on that flight.

Obviously, some of our surprises are far larger. But God never said He'd lead us around the valley of the shadow of death. He said He would go through it with us (Ps. 23:4, KJV), and He always does when we love Him and live our lives for His purpose. That's when God obligates Himself to make everything work for good.

James 1:2 says: "My brethren, count it all joy when you fall into various trials" (NKJV). Here's why. When we live our lives for God's purpose, it allows God to show off when we encounter trials. That's when your unwavering (no worries), wholehearted faith explodes, and your life is ignited with joy.

Nehemiah 8:10 tells us, "The joy of the LORD is your strength" (NKJV). Note it doesn't say your joy gives you strength. Did you know you can give God joy? Every time you follow God's nudge and move someone closer to the Lord, you give Him joy. And that gives you strength! That's a game changer for life!

Every time I follow God's nudge, I picture Jesus looking down on me with a big smile saying, "Way to go, Barry. You followed My lead, and you pulled it off!" And that always puts an extra bounce in my step. People often ask me why I'm so happy all the time. It's because I'm always just coming off one of these experiences and looking forward to the next one.

This is the starting line for having the time of your life, for the rest of your life!

SCRIPTURES FOR DEEPER REFLECTION

- **God's Word sets you free:** John 8:32 (NIV)

- **Enjoy this life with the understanding that it's temporary:** 2 Corinthians 4:18 (KJV)

- **Our time on earth is a nanosecond compared to eternity:** James 4:14 (NKJV)

- **All of us are going to stand before God:** Hebrews 9:27 (KJV)

- **We'll be rewarded in heaven forever for what we did on earth:** Matthew 16:27 (ESV)

- **Know that God is always with you through the good and the bad:** Hebrews 13:5 (NIV)

- **When you live for God's purpose, He delights in every detail of your life:** Psalm 37:23 (NLT)

- **God destroys worry when you love Him and live to seek and save the lost:** Romans 8:28 (NKJV)

- **The "first work" for every "first love" believer is sharing their faith:** Revelation 2:1–7 (NKJV)

- **Your job is to be a light in the darkness of this world:** Matthew 5:15 (KJV)

- **We don't believe the scriptures we know:** Matthew 18:3 (NIV)

- **God's eternal gift of salvation:** John 3:16 (NIV)

- **God wants to walk with you through your valleys without fear:** Psalm 23:4 (NKJV)

- **Trials ignite your faith:** James 1:2–3 (NKJV)

- **Giving God joy gives you strength:** Nehemiah 8:10 (NKJV)

CHAPTER 2

TO WHOM MUCH IS GIVEN

Luke 12:48 tells us, "To whom much was given, of him much will be required" (esv). That thought and obligation haunts me every day of my life, because I could never repay God for all He's given me. I am the most spiritually blessed person I know. It's no secret that I was born into a family business that God has blessed and prospered. But that's the small part of His blessings on my life.

It was 1901 when my granddad, Frank Meguiar Jr., started our family business making one bottle of polish at a time in the family garage. Even though Granddad had no chemical training, God directed him to formulate a polish that created a perfect finish on black lacquer furniture. He was so successful people started using his amazing "furniture polish" on their horseless carriages, which were all painted with black lacquer. More than half of all the horseless carriage manufacturers resided in Indiana, where he lived. Without his permission, Granddad's furniture polish became a carriage polish that led us to where we are today. It was all God!

By 1964 Meguiar's Car Wax had grown into a fifteen-thousand-square-foot building with twelve employees, almost all family, with gross sales of $600,000 a year, selling to car dealers and body shops by buffing cars with our polishes. My dad and his brothers were living the life, working half days, and had no interest in growing the business. After being their one-man accounting department during college, I was now full-time, and my desire to grow the business was not well received. They liked lazy afternoons.

Wearing a coat and tie, my sales calls across the country took me into the filthy garages of the car dealers and body shops of that day. Because my name was on the package, they figured I only had a job because my daddy hired me. So they would give me their worst car in the back of the garage to transform. And after I spent hours turning that car into a jewel, they would buy a gallon of this and a quart of that. It didn't take long for me to realize this was not the best use of my time for building a large business.

As a car guy from birth, I went to car shows on my travels across the United States and was shocked to discover that all the top show cars were being polished with our products. By 1964 just about every custom car painter in the country was using and recommending our products because of the perfect finishes they created. Our family's focus on the professional market opened the door for us to enter the retail marketplace.

That's when God inspired me to launch our products into the retail market focused on car guys. The demand was already there. But the family would have no part of it, seeing themselves as a professional brand and not wanting to get into what they called the "jippo/discount business." It was a hard sell that God would help me win with the depiction of car guys being pseudo professionals who don't care about price, will follow directions, and want the same results we do.

Peter Marshall Jr., the son of former US Senate Chaplain Peter Marshall, came to our church in those days with a strong message connecting God's great love for us with His allowing great challenges in our lives to perfect us. I remember how I thought God must not trust me enough to give me great challenges. I had no idea what lay ahead of me. I'll share those stories with you later.

Of far greater importance is my spiritual heritage. Exodus 20:6 tells us, "But I lavish unfailing love for a thousand generations on those who love me and obey my commands" (NLT). The key to this verse is the narrow focus of God's blessing on "those who love me and obey my commands." There are those in our family who share my heritage who did not obey God's commands. My heritage began with two Meguiar brothers who were given land grants in Franklin, Kentucky, for having fought in the Revolutionary War. Today, two Meguiar cemeteries remain in Franklin with tombstones of my family members going back to before the Civil War, all with scriptures inscribed on them. I have on my desk a well-worn book on systematic theology that belonged to Frank Meguiar Jr., my granddad and the founder of our family business.

My mother, Mabel Meguiar's, parents, Oscar and Nettie Hudson, both pastors, were two of the original founders of the Church of the Nazarene denomination at Pilot Point, Texas. They built churches all over America. Both were powerful preachers. They were the godliest people I've ever known, and I spent volumes of time with them growing up. My most powerful memories are of them kneeling by their bed after they retired for the evening, praying passionate prayers out loud for an hour. I can't wait to tell them about the impact they had on my life as my grandparents. What kind of impact are we having on our kids and grandkids?

I'm a living testimony to God's unfailing love extending down for generations to those who love Him and obey His commands. I saw it firsthand in my grandparents' lives and in the lives of my parents, Malcolm and Mabel Meguiar, whose lives were centered in their church. All of them made sure I was brought up in the ways of the Lord so that when I grew up, I did not depart from it.

THE BLESSING OF GODLY ROLE MODELS

In addition to my family heritage and having great churches and pastors all my life, I had a broad spectrum of godly friends and Karen right there with me all these years. God placed incredible mentors in our lives. I shudder to think where we would be today if they had not entered our lives. Hebrews 13:7 tells us to "Remember your leaders, who spoke the word of God to you. Consider the outcome of their way of life and imitate their faith." Paul encouraged young Timothy to "Set an example for the believers in speech, in conduct, in love, in faith and in purity" (1 Tim. 4:12). I was fortunate to have a few Timothies in my life. Dr. James Dobson is my longest-running mentor. We've been friends since I was fourteen, and I treasure our friendship. Just like Jesus, Jim has been the same yesterday and today and will be forever. He's the same guy now that I met as a kid. His steadfast, unwavering hold to the truth of God's

Word kept me from wavering when I might have wavered. Thank God for Jim Dobson!

In 1969 Karen and I moved from Pasadena to Irvine, California, with our small family business selling car wax to car dealers and body shops. Irvine was an off-the-radar community startup in Orange County. Land was dirt cheap, which made it a great place to buy a home and build a new factory. But we ended up without a church in the process and became "church bums." We were so hungry for the Word we were ready to go anywhere to hear a good sermon.

On a rainy Friday night, September 11, 1970, we drove over an hour to hear an evangelist in Covina, California. The church was electric with the presence of God. We had never seen anything like it, and we soaked it in. After the incredible service, we had to go outside the church to see what kind of a church it was. The sign read "Covina First Assembly." Being Nazarenes, we were anti-Pentecostals! Had we known it was an Assemblies of God church, we never would have gone to that church. God has a sense of humor!

We ended up going to Santa Ana First Assembly that next Sunday morning, September 13, 1970, and on almost every Sunday morning, Sunday night, and Wednesday night thereafter for the next thirty-one years. I was eventually awarded Layman of the Year at the Assemblies of God General Council, served on their World Missions Board and Seminary Board, and led lay ministries for the Assemblies for two years. When you follow God's lead, you have no idea where He'll take you.

On that first morning at Santa Ana (Orange County) First Assembly, we met most of the closest friends we have today, fifty years later. We've gone from no kids together, to kids, to grandkids, to sharing joys and tragedies and losses and experiences that have bonded us together forever. What a gift it is to know you have a circle of friends there for you, no matter what happens, loving you and holding you in prayer. The gift of Christian friends is among the most priceless. We have an overabundance.

We also met Gwen Wilkerson, the wife of David Wilkerson, on that first morning. David Wilkerson was the founder of

Teen Challenge, author of the huge best seller *The Cross and the Switchblade*, and ultimately pastor of Times Square Church in New York City at 51st and Broadway. Dave and Gwen are now waiting for us in heaven.

Two months earlier, David had purchased a house in Florida, only to back out of it a couple of weeks later. When the real estate agent asked why, David said, "The Lord told me I'm supposed to move to Irvine, California." How did this prophet living in New York City even know about tiny, off-the-radar Irvine? Yet he moved his family from New York City to Irvine, two blocks from our house. And he would later say it was to meet us. We didn't even know who David Wilkerson was. Two years later he moved his ministry to Dallas, and we spent the next forty years of our lives commuting to be with them in Dallas and New York City and in crusades across America.

For forty years we were best friends with Dave and Gwen Wilkerson. There's no question we would not be where we are today spiritually without their influence on our lives. I would sit for hours listening to Dave and people like Leonard Ravenhill discussing deep theological thoughts, and I would wonder how I got there. I'm just a peddler of car wax. Proverbs 13:20 says, "Whoever walks with the wise becomes wise, but the companion of fools will suffer harm" (ESV). I knew the Lord was preparing me, but for what I had no idea.

Years later Dave and I, along with a real estate agent, went looking for a theater in NYC to buy for Times Square Church. We discovered the Mark Hellinger Theatre. It was the flagship of Broadway theaters, which had fallen on hard times. The price was way beyond our reach. But that night, like most nights, Dave spent two to three hours in prayer, and God told him that night He would give him that church. Dave ended up paying cash. I love this quote from Dave: "Before I try to attempt anything for God, I've got to come out of His presence. I've got to come out with something I've received in His presence that is changing me. I have been changed. I have not gotten this in a seminary. I have not gotten this from man. I got this alone with Jesus, beholding His face."

My point is this: when God brings David Wilkerson into your

life for forty years, it transforms your life, and you know it's a gift from God. I've been entrusted with spiritual wealth all my life. As time went on I realized, as it was happening, that God was preparing me to help others learn how to have an intimate relationship with Him. And I knew if I buried the talent, what I had received would be taken away from me. There was no chance I was going to let that happen.

After a lifetime of God blessing me with far more than I deserve, He owns me! Everything I am and have belongs to Him. I'm well aware of my age, and I know I could die tomorrow. And if that should happen, I want to be in full stride trying to reach one more person for the Lord. I can honestly tell you that I've never felt better, had more energy, felt freer, or been more excited to wake up every day to see what God has in store for me for that day! In short, my life could not be more ignited! But this book is not about me. It's about you and how effortlessly you can step into an intimate relationship with God that you've never known existed. All it requires of you is to act on God's Word with the faith of a little child. This is not new theology. It's Bible 101.

HE OWNS ME

Are you ready?

SCRIPTURES FOR DEEPER REFLECTION

- **The more we know about God, the more that's required of us:** Luke 12:48 (ESV)

- **God's blessings flow down for generations to those who obey Him:** Exodus 20:6 (NLT)

- **Praise God for those who got you where you are spiritually:** Hebrews 13:7 (NIV)

- **Set an example for everyone watching you—move everyone closer to Jesus:** 1 Timothy 4:12 (NIV)

- **Choose your friends carefully:** Proverbs 13:20 (ESV)

CHAPTER 3

HAPPINESS VERSUS JOY

PEOPLE THINK I never lose my joy because I've had a Polly-anna life with a beautiful wife and family, cool cars, and a great business—living the dream. And they're partly right. I never lose my joy, but it's for totally different reasons than they perceive. God has allowed me to go through massive challenges in my life so I could have firsthand knowledge of His faithfulness, which I get to share with people almost every day.

It's a choice! I have longtime, close friends who have loved and served the Lord all their lives. But they've allowed the world to replace their joy with fear and to age them greatly. Proverbs 17:22 says it well: "A cheerful heart is good medicine, but a broken spirit saps a person's strength" (NLT).

It's the proverbial chicken and the egg concept where each part leads to the next. Because I love God and love to share my faith, God makes everything in my life work for good. That's His promise. And that builds my faith, increases my joy, and expands my excitement to share my faith. And it gets better every time I do it! Once you make the commitment to move everyone, every day, closer to Jesus, the opportunities abound. Even a spilled cup of coffee becomes a faith-sharing opportunity.

In the naiveté of my early marriage/small business/small faith days, I questioned God on everything. I even got upset when people I shared my faith with didn't get saved on the spot. I'm so thankful that God has a sense of humor and is full of grace—or I would have been toast!

I couldn't understand why God allowed bad things to happen and why I should count it all joy (Jas. 1:2). I had no idea how He uses the bad things in our lives to perfect us, draw us closer to Him, open new opportunities to share our faith, and enlarge what we have to share. First Peter 1:6–7 explains how "pure gold put through the fire comes out of it proved pure; genuine faith put through this suffering comes out proved genuine" (MSG).

I learned early on that a growing faith through dark times is often rewarded with darker times and more growth. As the song title goes, "Nobody Knows the Trouble I've Seen"—and it's so true! Only God knows the dark times I've experienced without losing my joy, because I knew He was right there with me. *Yea, though I walk through the valley of the shadow of death...*

Hallelujah!

JOY IN THE DARKNESS

It was because of our earlier trials that we kept our joy in the midst of our darkest hour when we lost Nicole, our beloved forty-nine-year-old daughter. I shed half the tears of my lifetime coming to grips with the harsh reality of her loss. But I never questioned God or lost my joy.

Nicole was a faith-sharing machine. So many people have told us their stories of how God directed Nicole to them in the midst of their struggles. What they didn't know was the depth of Nicole's struggles that drove her to her knees in her "war room" prayer closet ferociously seeking God's comfort and direction. And every time she resurfaced, she exploded onto the scene with razor-sharp focus and all the right scriptures to reach the hurting people around her that no one knew were hurting.

We can't begin to estimate how many people she led to the Lord in her lifetime, and then through her memorial service (more than a thousand people attended) and via the video of her memorial service—"Nicole Meguiar's Celebration of Life"— which has been viewed by more than eleven thousand people on YouTube. It's the real-life version of what I'm telling you now. (You can watch the YouTube video here: https://www.youtube.com/watch?v=jlechLjOvrM.)

I see her smiling face in a hot rod on my phone every day. And every time I see it, I think to myself, "She's even happier now." And that makes me happy.

If the Word of God doesn't work during our darkest hours, it's worthless. But it does, every time. The Bible is intimately relevant in every situation, from the point of martyrdom to the pinnacle of success. God is always there speaking to you and drawing you closer to Him when you love Him and use everything this world throws at you to share your faith and increase your joy.

If you take nothing else away from this book, please hear this admonition: don't let anything rob you of your joy! Never lose your joy. And you never will when you bear fruit. "By this My Father is glorified, that you bear much fruit: so you will be My disciples.... These things I have spoken to you, that My joy may remain in you, and that your joy may be full" (John 15:8, 11, NKJV). Are you hearing this? When you live your life for God's purpose, when your life is begetting new Christians, God is promising you that *your* joy will be full every day!

In stark contrast, happiness is fleeting. Most of us are happy and unhappy every day, depending on what's happening at the moment. I made the sale; I lost the sale. It was a great meal or a bad meal. Even the homeless can be happy or unhappy depending on whether they find a meal or a warm place to sleep. Happiness is relative, fleeting, and circumstantial.

Joy is an entirely different animal because it has nothing to do with circumstances and everything to do with your intimacy with God. No matter how good or bad your day has been, it can't rob you of your joy when your joy comes from God. In fact, God told us to not be surprised by the trials we encounter. "I have told you all this so that you may have peace in me. Here on earth you will have many trials and sorrows. But take heart, because I have overcome the world" (John 16:33, NLT).

The deeper truth is how God uses the bad stuff to perfect us. One of my many character flaws has been lack of patience. I was the one who told God I want patience—and I want it right now! So that's an area God had to give added attention to in my life, by not giving me what I wanted on demand. "Knowing this, that the trying of your faith worketh patience. But let patience have her perfect work, that ye may be perfect and entire, wanting nothing" (Jas. 1:3–4, KJV).

When we were first married, Karen and I volunteered for everything possible in our desire to show God how much we loved Him and to earn His love for us. Mind you, there's nothing scriptural in either one of those desires. There's nothing we can do to earn more of God's love because He loves us all completely.

Eventually, in the flurry of our well-doing and sacrifice, we realized that we had no joy. In fact, we were so weary it was affecting our relationship. So we began praying specifically for joy in our lives. Not long after, our church celebrated its fiftieth anniversary with a luncheon that had Governor Ronald Reagan's legal affairs secretary, Herb Ellingwood, as the luncheon speaker.

God is so amazing. Although I didn't have any responsibilities at that luncheon, God sat me at the head table, right beside Herb Ellingwood. And during that next hour, before he spoke, Herb forever changed my life. Through tears and laughter, he told me one story after another about his continuous faith-sharing experiences. I walked away from that conversation in tears, telling God I wanted what Herb had: "I want that joy!"

That's what launched Karen and me into being full-time faith sharers and our ministry of Ignite America. After I find my mom and dad in heaven, and our daughter Nicole, I'm making a beeline to find Herb Ellingwood! I can't wait to tell him of all the lives that have been changed because he took the time to share with me the joy that comes from sharing your faith.

Before we knew it, our lives were full of joy. It was after that when we discovered John 15:11, telling us how sharing our faith will make our joy full. Can you imagine what went through our minds when we read that scripture for the first time with understanding, after experiencing it firsthand?

BEWARE!

I need to give you a warning. Beware of making anything other than God your "first love" (Rev. 2:4, NKJV). Never let your prayers be filled with asking God to help you with something/anything! Because whatever that thing is involves people who will always let you down. And when your prayers are focused on anything other than God, that thing becomes your god—and you find yourself asking God to help you with your god. It may be something He doesn't even want you to do or doesn't want to bless as long as you're basing your joy on it rather than on Him! Proverbs 3:5 reminds us to seek the Lord with our whole heart and not rely on our own thought processes. The key to having your life filled with joy is your steadfast commitment to keeping God as your first love and living for His purpose. When God is your first love you'll do the "first works" (v. 4), which is to tell people about Jesus. That's when God makes *everything* in your life work for good, *and* you'll never lose your joy again!

I know we're instructed to take our petitions to God, and we often *have not because we ask not.* (See James 4:2–3.) But in times of trouble I often tell God, "I ask You for nothing because of Romans 8:28: You know I live for Your purpose, and I know You keep Your Word." He already knows the severity of my struggles, the strength of my faith, my requests before I make them, and the desires of my heart. And Psalm 37:4 tells us to "delight yourself in the LORD, and he will give you the desires of your heart" (ESV). I prefer to thank God in advance for how He's going to solve my problems. And you can do that when you're living your life for His purpose. That's another game changer!

The problem comes when we predetermine where we think the Lord is supposed to take us. That's when I've gotten myself in trouble. How many times when I've been in trouble has Karen asked me, "Did you pray about this?" I hate it when she does that!

Isaiah 55:8–9 tells us: "'For my thoughts are not your thoughts, neither are your ways my ways,' declares the LORD."

God has a huge advantage over you. He knows everything, and you know nothing by comparison. You see what you believe to be good in the short term, but He knows what's good for you in the long term. It may not make you happy when He allows you to go through the fires of life, but that's how He perfects your faith.

GOD HAS A HUGE ADVANTAGE

Never let the hard things in your life rob you of your joy. When you live for God's purpose and allow Him to direct your steps, everything that happens to you will be allowed or ordained by God to prepare you for eternity. "For you know that when your faith is tested, your endurance has a chance to grow. So let it grow, for when your endurance is fully developed, you will be perfect and complete, needing nothing" (Jas. 1:3–4, NLT). This is why God tells us to "count it all joy" (v. 2, NKJV).

And it gets better and better with every faith-sharing experience as you grow closer and closer to God with the Holy Spirit nudging you into action. But that's when you become a high-priority target for Satan. When serious things begin to go wrong, it may be Satan attempting to distract or discourage you from staying on track with God. Always know this: "Greater is he that is in you [God], than he [Satan] that is in the world" (1 John 4:4, KJV).

When bad things happen that I'm convinced are caused by Satan messing with me, it drives me closer to God because I know what Satan means for evil, God uses for good (Gen. 50:20). That's basic Scripture and another game changer for your life. Seriously!

I've often heard the phrase "They're so heavenly minded they're of no earthly good." It's like, don't go near happy people who love God and their neighbors as themselves and want to help you. The truth is, heavenly minded people are the only hope for this world. And from our side of the equation, as Christians, we should always be ready and eager for God to speak through us to the needs of those around us (1 Pet. 3:15). That keeps you on your toes and God-focused.

To be continually filled with the joy of the Lord in the midst of darkness may be life's greatest confirmation that God is real!

SCRIPTURES FOR DEEPER REFLECTION

- **Caving in to the cares of this world saps your strength:** Proverbs 17:22 (NLT)

- **When things go bad, know that God is up to something:** James 1:2–4 (ESV)

- **Most salvations and spiritual growth spurts happen when things go bad:** 1 Peter 1:6–7 (MSG)

- **Bearing fruit (new Christians) is the key to never losing your joy:** John 15:8–11 (NKJV)

- **Joy gives you peace in the midst of trials and sorrows:** John 16:33 (NLT)

- **Sharing your faith leads to joy, which leads to peace, which leads to patience:** James 1:3–4 (KJV)

- **Never let anything distract your focus on God:** Revelation 2:4 (NKJV)

- **God always honors wholehearted faith and dependence:** Proverbs 3:5–6 (NKJV)

- **Prayers asking for God's will are always answered:** James 4:2–3 (NKJV)

- **God answers your prayers when you love Him and live for Him:** Romans 8:28 (NKJV)

- **When God is your "first love," your desires are His desires:** Psalm 37:4 (NKJV)

- **You would answer your prayers the same way God answers your prayers if you knew what He knows:** Isaiah 55:8–9 (NIV)

- **If God is for you, who can be against you?** 1 John 4:4 (KJV)

- **It's a good thing when bad things happen:** Genesis 50:20 (ESV)

- **Always being ready keeps your focus on God:** 1 Peter 3:15 (MEV)

CHAPTER 4

THE END OF WORRY

OW EASILY WE read and quote scriptures and then ignore them without giving it a second thought. Here's an example: Proverbs 3:5 tells us to "trust in the LORD with all your heart…and he will make your paths straight." Most Christians know, believe, and quote this scripture. But it's almost impossible to find a Christian who actually trusts God with their whole heart—which is the entire basis of our relationship with God. We're called "people of faith," and without faith it's impossible to please God (Heb. 11:6).

It's impossible to be in sync with God when you're not trusting Him with your whole heart and unwavering faith. James 1:6–8 says: "Be sure that your faith is in God alone. Do not waver, for a person with divided loyalty is as unsettled as a wave of the sea that is blown and tossed by the wind. Such people should not expect to receive anything from the Lord…they are unstable in everything they do" (NLT). If you're praying and worrying at the same time, you can't expect God to answer your prayers.

Here's a self-test: If you knew you were about to lose your job, or the doctors told you that you were dying or that your daughter just died, what would be your first reaction? If your honest answer is fear, you'd be in good company. Over 80 percent of all Americans, including Christians, are already living in fear without having any of these issues.[1] But that's not scriptural, and it's not how God wants you to live your life. Trusting God with your whole heart obliterates fear.

On a personal basis, my faith never wavered when I faced all these issues and many, many more. While that may seem like extreme faith, I did it automatically—without even trying. That's the underlying message of this book. And it will ignite your life! You can have wholehearted faith effortlessly by simply following basic biblical truths that you already know and quote. It's not complicated.

Trusting God with your whole heart becomes automatic when God is your first love and you're doing the first work of telling people about Him. The first thing every new believer does is tell people about Jesus: "I was blind but now I see!" (John 9:25). But God never intended that to be a one-time experience. God created you to be His spokesman! Jeremiah 1:5 tells us: "Before I formed you in the womb I knew you, before you were born I set you apart; I appointed you as a prophet to the nations."

Throughout the Bible, God explains that loving Him cannot be disconnected from loving others as ourselves, being as concerned for their salvation as we are for our own. When God is your first love, you'll do the first work—telling people about Him, the first thing every new Christian does. The things we love the most, we talk about the most. Consider this: when God loves us, He's "salvationing" us! God's love is entirely and completely consumed and razor-focused on our salvation! He created us to spend eternity with Him. And when we love on others, we're "salvationing" them. Better yet, He's "salvationing" them through us as His Holy Spirit speaks to them through us and draws them to Himself. It's sacred!

I know it sounds too easy, but it's true. You can have whole-hearted faith simply by believing the scriptures you already know and acting on them. Matthew 18:3 goes so far as to say: "Unless you change and become like little children [with childlike faith], you will never enter the kingdom of heaven." Trusting God with your whole heart comes automatically when you believe His Word with childlike faith and live your life accordingly.

With all that's going on in the world, it's past time to take personal responsibility for your relationship with God. Limiting your spiritual growth to twenty-minute, feel-good Sunday morning sermons telling you how to be a better person is paralyzing. If that's your Sunday experience, you need to find a pastor who will get you off the bench and into God's plan for your life—to fulfill His purpose.

Here's the bottom line: you can't trust God in your own strength! I've heard a lifetime of messages on trusting God. Just trust God!

When you're having a problem, everyone tells you to trust God. It sounds so righteous and so spiritual. But trusting God wholeheartedly in your own strength is impossible. You'll fail every time. If you were able to trust God enough in your own strength to bring a miracle, the pride of doing that miracle would probably destroy you. God knows that.

And then there are the raised voices of saints yelling, "We trust You, God!" as if the volume of their voices has more influence on God than the content of their hearts. Clearly the "effectual fervent prayer of a righteous man availeth much" (Jas. 5:16, KJV), but only if the voice matches the heart's intent. Otherwise, it's a clanging cymbal.

NEVER LIFT!

Most of us know the phrase "pedal to the metal." It refers to pushing the accelerator of your car down to the metal as far as it will go. But there's another car guy term that's lesser known by non-car guys. It's called "never lift." "Never lift" refers to never lifting the pedal off the metal when you're racing. When you lift off the accelerator, you can expect to be passed. Thus, the euphemistic phrase among car guys is to "Never lift!"

NEVER LIFT!

So why do race car drivers lift their feet off the accelerator? It's called fear! When they approach an area of the racecourse that may exceed their driving skill, they lift out of fear. That's lack of trust! And that's when the more experienced drivers pass them with no fear. The great drivers never lift out of fear.

Do you want to be a great Christian? This same dynamic applies to your spiritual life and says volumes about where you are spiritually. When bad news comes, does fear cause you to lift off the accelerator of your life, or do you have wholehearted faith that allows you to "never lift"? God expects you to trust Him with *your whole heart*, no matter what this world throws at you. First John 4:18 explains, "Such love has no fear, because perfect love expels all fear" (NLT).

That's an entirely different way of living and where God wants you to live your life every day. Mind you, living your life without fear is a greatly disputed fact, even among pastors I esteem. But God says "Fear Not" 365 times in the Bible. Why would God taunt you with His promise to answer your prayers and direct your steps when you trust Him with your whole heart if it wasn't possible? God wouldn't do that. His nature of pure truth wouldn't allow Him to do that. So it's definitely true. But how do you get there?

When you trust God with your whole heart in all areas of your life, life is a whole lot easier. "Do not be anxious about anything, but in every situation, by prayer and petition, with thanksgiving, present your requests to God. And the peace of God, which tran-scends all understanding, will guard your hearts and your minds in Christ Jesus" (Phil. 4:6). Again, this is just basic Scripture. And this is how God intends for you to live every day of your life. Who knew that sharing your faith is what opens the door to having whole-hearted faith?

After my dad passed away, my uncle and his two sons opposed me in every way possible. They didn't want to be in the retail market even though we had become the top-selling car wax in America. So they sold their shares of our family business to a joint venture capi-talist. And after five years, my joint venture partner seized control of my board and planned to throw me out of my company the next morning via a conference call board meeting. It was devastating news. I was sixty-five years old—too late to start over. I was losing my income, my hundred-year-old family business, my reputation, and most importantly, my testimony. Where's Barry's God now?

It was the end of my life as I knew it, and I was powerless to do anything about it. But I never lifted. That's when God has you right where He wants you. If you're at that point right now, here's God's message to you: "My grace is sufficient for you, for my power is made perfect in weakness" (2 Cor. 12:9). There's nothing God can't do!

The worst times in our lives are the best times to learn who God is and know we can trust Him wholeheartedly! I know that's the opposite of what you're thinking right now. You're thinking your situation is unique and there's no way out, but there's always a way out when you trust God with your whole heart. This is the $64,000 question of your life: Do you trust God with your whole heart?

Here's how I handled the worst night of my life up until that time. As bad as this was, God was preparing me for a bigger challenge still ahead of me. I only prayed a short prayer that night. I almost didn't pray at all. The night before I was being thrown out of my business and my life appeared to be over, I told God, "I ask You for nothing. I'm good, because of two things: You know I live for Your purpose, and I know You keep Your Word [to make everything work for good]."

That wasn't mind-over-matter blind faith, and it wasn't faith in my own strength calling out to God. It was simple childlike faith, in the quiet of my bedroom that night, believing and acting on God's promise in Romans 8:28 to make it all work for good—if you live your life for His purpose. You may have missed that part. John 8:32 tells us: "You will know the truth, and the truth will set you free." The simple truth of God's Word sets us free from worry and allows us to have wholehearted faith effortlessly and automatically, even in the darkest moments of our lives.

It bears repeating: we know and quote scriptures that we convince ourselves we believe, but we don't believe them. If we did believe them, all our lives would be miraculous and America would be bursting with revival.

This is what wholehearted faith looks like! It could not have been easier for me. After my short prayer, I went right to sleep, slept soundly all night, and woke up the next morning refreshed and excited to see what God was going to do. I knew He was up to something. I wish you could have been there. Less than ten minutes into our board meeting, God destroyed my joint venture partner's plans, and I couldn't help but break out laughing inside. At the worst moment of my life, when I was powerless, God did the impossible! That's what "never lift" faith looks like in the real world.

Why would you not want to get in on this?

SCRIPTURES FOR DEEPER REFLECTION

- **Most Christians know and quote this scripture without living it:** Proverbs 3:5 (NIV)

- **"First love" Christians doing the "first work" are people of faith!** Hebrews 11:6 (NIV)

- **Fear of man is the opposite of faith in God:** James 1:6–8 (NLT)

- **You can't stop new believers from sharing their faith because God is their first love:** John 9:25 (NIV)

- **From birth, God created you to be His spokesperson:** Jeremiah 1:5 (NIV)

- **Your "walk" has to match your "talk" for your words to have power:** James 5:16 (KJV)

- **God expects us to live without fear and to "never lift":** 1 John 4:18 (NLT)

- **God rewards "first love" Christians doing the first work with supernatural peace:** Philippians 4:6–7 (NIV)

- **God loves to show off during the worst moments of our lives:** 2 Corinthians 12:9 (NIV)

- **Live for God's purpose and He'll work all things for your good:** Romans 8:28 (NKJV)

- **The simple truth of God's Word sets us free from worry:** John 8:32 (NLT)

CHAPTER 5

WHERE THE RUBBER MEETS THE ROAD

WHEN I FIRST started feeling the Holy Spirit's nudge to go into retail, I knew nothing about the retail market. One thing I knew for sure: the challenge was way bigger than me, and only God could pull it off.

We moved our home and business to Irvine, California, in 1969, before it became a city. I was traveling all over the country, calling on accounts, while God kept building this retail thing inside me. God was giving me glimpses of what was going to happen, but I didn't know how to get there. I knew I needed help. So I prayed, "God, I know You're leading me into the retail market, and You know I need help." I knew and relied on Matthew 6:8, which assures us that God always knows exactly what we need before we ask.

Not long after that I was in a waiting room at an account in Dallas with other traveling salesmen, and there was a well-dressed man sitting next to me about twenty-five years my senior. We struck up a conversation until he went to his buyer and I went to mine. Two weeks later I walked into another waiting room of an account in Seattle, and there was the same guy. His name was Craig Benson. Now mind you, I already knew there are no coincidences when you're living your life for God's purpose. I knew God was up to something. Now our conversation was going beyond the pleasantries.

When he asked what I was working on, I explained that the passion I had was not why I was in that room: "I have a dream of taking the 'Best car wax in the world' into the consumer market—and I don't have a clue what I'm doing." To this he responded, "Oh, I can help you with that." It turned out he was a general partner in the largest ad agency in the country.

I said that would be great, but I didn't have any money. Then he asked where I lived, and we discovered we lived about ten minutes from each other. Do you get the picture? We met in Dallas and then Seattle and lived ten minutes apart from each other in California. And then God did the impossible. We had lunch when we got back home, and then Craig started coming over to my house one night a week, spending two hours at a time mentoring me for free. He ended up giving me the equivalent of a master's degree in marketing and entering the consumer marketplace. Only God!

Next I met a high-powered ad guy at a reception in Los Angeles. His name was Al Atherton, and his ad agency, Atherton-Privett, created the famous Hawaiian Punch TV ads featuring the cartoon character "Punchy." After hearing my story, he said he could help me, and I again explained, "I don't have any money."

But he was intrigued with my story, my passion, and my naiveté and asked where my office was. When I said Irvine, he said, "I'll be down there next week. I'll stop by." That started months of his driving down to Irvine every week, asking only for a Coke to drink with his sack lunch. He bought a Ferrari during our tenure and, not wanting to wait for shipping, had his new Ferrari flown over from Italy. God inspired this exceedingly wealthy and successful advertising executive to counsel this kid with a dream, and he asked for nothing. This is how God directs your steps when you're following His lead.

If it were not for outside board members, I never would have gained permission to take Meguiar's into the retail market. The family was completely against me. But because of our outside, non-family board members, I won most of my critical board votes by one vote.

The biggest marketing challenge of all was to create our new image for the retail market. I had to stay far away from the Mirror Glaze branding of our professional products. Our actual company name was Mirror Bright Polish Company. Early on in our company history, my granddad's pastor came by to see him testing his products on a black car. And he remarked, "That's a mirror-bright finish."

And my granddad said, "That's it. That's what I'm going to call my company: the Mirror Bright Polish Company."

Now, it was 1970. We had just landed on the moon, and every package designer was focused on space-age graphics. I had to choose between using the name Mirror Bright, which is very descriptive of what our products do, or the name Meguiar's, which no one could read or pronounce. The decision seemed obvious, but God nudged me to go with Meguiar's. And this one package designer told me I should emphasize the heritage of our seventy-year-old family business with a retro logo. That would break all the trends and the advice of every other designer I interviewed. Back in 1970, we threw away everything that was old, even old race cars. Antiquing came in after that period. But the designer's idea seemed right to me.

Because my family members were totally against going retail, I was given only a small budget from our board of directors for the project. That night I called the designer at his studio asking for a quote and emphasizing that we had limited funds. He asked for fifteen minutes, and while he calculated I prayed. I had a sense of the enormity of this decision and the unanimous disapproval I would get for going retro before retro was cool. So I told God I absolutely, positively needed His guidance on this one. I asked Him to have the designer's quote come in over the budget if he was the wrong guy and under the budget if he was the right guy.

When he called me back, his quote was—to the dollar—the same amount of the budget given to me that morning. That's when I told God, "OK, I'm absolutely all in! I'm following Your lead from now on." And I have. We were an invisible company doing $750,000 in gross sales at that time. Now the Meguiar's brand is known and respected by almost every person in the world who uses car wax. Following God's lead has some perks!

In November 1973, I launched Meguiar's into the consumer market. You might say it was a daunting task for a young guy who had never sold anything into the retail market and had a family full of doubters wanting me to fail. But I felt God's nudge firmly on my back, and I was determined to follow His lead—having no idea God was going to propel us into being the top-selling car wax in America.

By 1976 we were gaining traction, and I was in dire need of seasoned marketing experience. I began interviewing agencies, and all of them were outside my comfort zone in lifestyle. One day I received a call from a young man representing an agency called Something Good Is Going to Happen. Because the biggest Christian TV show at the time had that name, I knew they were Christians.

I asked him, "How fast can you come?" And he said, "Right now." I couldn't wait. When I hung up that phone, I shouted for joy, "Thank You, God! I knew You'd provide the right guy for me." But once we met, five minutes into the conversation, I knew he was the wrong guy and encouraged him to leave. At that point I got mad at God. In fact, I yelled at Him. I literally shouted, "After all I've done for You, why are You doing this to me?" Thank God He has a sense of humor and gives us grace. I was being so stupid.

About two weeks later I received a call from Dick Koeth, who told me he was the owner of Something Good Is Going to Happen. He said he'd had a guy doing some cold calls who didn't work out, and he was following up. I asked him how quickly he could come, and he said, "Right now." This time I waited with zero enthusiasm, and within five minutes of his coming in the door, I knew he was a gift from God.

My executive team (who became like family to me) and I spent the next forty years together building Meguiar's into the top-selling car wax in America and in countries around the world. God, in His loving and patient mentoring of me, honed me to know that even when things take an unexpected left turn, He's right there. "Do not be anxious about anything, but in every situation, by prayer and petition, with thanksgiving, present your requests to God. And the peace of God, which transcends all understanding, will guard your hearts and your minds in Christ Jesus" (Phil. 4:6–7). This is such an important scripture!

SOMETHING DEEPER

Yet there's a deeper level of faith that needs to be addressed here. Millions of Christians around the world worship God and go to church knowing it could cost them their lives. They're fearless and full of joy. I've seen them face-to-face and wanted to have the joy they had even in the darkness of their world, because of their darkness. You see, they have nowhere to turn. Without the persecution, they may have been nominal Christians. But because they have nowhere to run, they have to place wholehearted trust in God, and that's when God obligates Himself to supply our needs. "Trust in the LORD with all your heart...and He will direct your paths" (Prov. 3:5–6, MEV).

The options for the persecuted church are all but nonexistent. If they are to serve God, their only option is to trust Him with their whole hearts to protect them, keep them out of prison, and put food on their tables. Seeing that level of trust firsthand convicted me. I felt like I was the impoverished one. My dependence on God and my joy were nowhere close to what I was seeing in those persecuted believers. They were ignited!

I WANT WHAT THEY HAVE

I'm reminded of a beloved Ukrainian pastor, a survivor of World War II, who told me of how he saw the glory of God as his Russian guards beat him and left him to die. Of all the wonderful things he did as a pastor, he said that was when he felt closest to God. And his prayer was not to escape but for God to raise him back up so he could prove to those guards that his God was real—and God answered his prayer!

I came home asking God, "How can I have that kind of dependence on You and that joy without living in their peril? Is it possible to trust You for everything in America, where there's an abundance of everything?" If you hunger for this kind of relationship with God, you're going to enjoy where this book is taking you. You're about to learn how easy it is to trust God for everything in your life no matter what the future holds.

Looking at both worlds through God's eyes, the poverty-and-persecution model seems to be working exceedingly better than the peace-and-prosperity model of America. While the church is imploding in America, it's exploding everywhere Christians are persecuted. And from that perspective, it's a small step to conclude that God is allowing the current destruction of America to encourage Americans to begin trusting Him with their whole hearts.

Most unbelievers are now keenly aware that our world is out of control and are hoping there's a God who can end the chaos,[1] are looking for someone to talk to about God,[2] and already have at least one Christian in their life that they trust.[3] "Lift up your eyes and look on the fields, for they are already white for harvest!" (John 4:35, NKJV). We could ignite revival in America in thirty days if we ourselves were ignited. That's why I'm writing this book.

This is a powerful message to the millions of people who are living in darkness and poverty and threat of life in America right now. If you're among the less fortunate in America, you can far more easily identify with God being your only hope than those with great wealth. In that respect, you have a great advantage because you have far more to gain from trusting the God who made you, loves you, has a plan for your life (Jer. 29:11), and wants you to spend eternity with Him. And sharing your faith from less fortunate circumstances is far more powerful than it is from someone who doesn't understand what it takes to trust God, because they're in need of nothing. That's why Matthew 19:24 explains, "It is easier for a camel to go through the eye of a needle than for someone who is rich to enter the kingdom of God."

This takes us back to the vast difference between knowing Scripture and living it out in your own life. American Christians are great at believing scriptures they don't live and ultimately misinterpret. Small wonder that only 51 percent of pastors, 21 percent of Evangelicals, and 6 percent of Americans still hold the biblical worldview of heaven and hell and believe Jesus is the only way to heaven.[4] We know the Scriptures, but we don't believe the Scriptures!

There's no question that God obligated Himself to bless us when we have wholehearted faith. The question remains, How do we get there? How can we have unwavering, wholehearted faith? I'm about to tell you, and it's going to ignite your life.

SCRIPTURES FOR DEEPER REFLECTION

- **God knows your needs before you request His help:** Matthew 6:8 (NLT)

- **Fear is overrated:** Philippians 4:6–7 (NIV)

- **Fear cancels God's self-imposed obligation to direct your steps:** Proverbs 3:5–6 (MEV)

- **No matter where you are, God has plans for you:** Jeremiah 29:11 (NIV)

- **There has never been an easier time to lead people to Jesus:** John 4:35 (NKJV)

- **The less you have, the easier it is to depend on God:** Matthew 19:24 (NIV)

CHAPTER 6

PRIMED FOR IGNITION

MOST PEOPLE KNOW me as the car guy who loves perfectly restored old cars, like the black '57 Chevy that was my first car and the one I dated Karen in. I recently presented Detroit Autorama's famous Ridler Award to an insanely beautiful '31 Chevy that sat out in a doorless barn for twenty years. It only took twenty-thousand man-hours and two million dollars to bring it back. I can't say enough about this car, its owners, and the team that built it. You can't get any better. But watching God restore people is a thousand times more exciting because it's eternal.

I received a call from a friend telling me a longtime mutual friend of ours was dying. I hadn't seen him in years. From his hospice bed, he told his wife he wanted to talk to me, so she called the person who was calling me. I knew exactly what he wanted to talk about. Karen and I were heading to a movie, so I asked her to drive while I made the call. In that short drive I led my dying friend to the Lord. It took about twelve minutes! But it was forty years of chumming, sowing seeds into his life, seemingly without effect, that made that possible. Can you imagine my excitement at the end of that call? Never give up on people!

As I said earlier, as passionate as I am about my business, it's not going to matter how many bottles of car wax I sold when I get to heaven. The only thing that will matter is how many people are in heaven because of my influence. You see, it's not one or the other. For the last sixty years I could not have been more passionate about my business or worked harder to make it a success. And I haven't lost an ounce of that excitement. I thank God every day for the privilege of being part of my family business, working with great people, and doing my dad and granddad proud. Being a car guy is the icing on the cake! But there has not been one degree of separation between my business life and my devotion to moving everyone I meet, every day, closer to Jesus.

There's no greater joy, and no better way to ignite your life, than to witness God using you to ignite faith in the lives of those around you. Here's the best news of all. The entire world is primed for ignition. Over 80 percent of the unchurched would like to believe there's a God who can make sense out of today's chaos, and they are looking for someone to tell them who that God is—to ignite them! They don't know it, but they're desperate for what you have— to know there's a God who loves them and wants to protect them and give them His gift of eternal life. Most everyone around you wants to escape the fear and darkness closing in on them, and you may be their only way out. Just a simple God-referencing comment can grab the attention of those most hurting. Jesus said, "Follow Me, and I will make you become fishers of men" (Mark 1:17, NASB).

People are hurting, and no one cares. That's why it's a big event when you care enough to stop and listen and love on them— allowing God to love them through you. Jesus said, "By this all will know that you are My disciples, if you have love for one another" (John 13:35, NKJV). You'll be amazed how fast complete strangers will share their deepest concerns with you as the Holy Spirit confirms the genuineness of your love for them. Always remember that God is "salvationing" us when He loves us, and He's "salvationing" others through us when we love on them.

During the writing of this book, Karen and I were out of town attending the funeral of a close friend. While grabbing a bite to eat at a local restaurant, we asked our server, as we do most servers, if she had anything we could pray for her about. This is entry-level faith sharing 101. Anyone can do this. Just think of how often you're being served by someone who is most likely hurting and in need of prayer.

The key is to get the server's name when they first arrive at your table, then build a relationship while the order is being taken, and then end by adding one more question: Is there anything I can pray for you about? Most of the time you'll get a serious, if not emotional, response. Again, almost everyone is hurting and believes no one cares. And when people are hurting, they never turn down prayers.

Even when they say no, it still works. Just say, "Then we'll thank God for giving you such a wonderful life!" You never want to make anyone uncomfortable. Their guardedness tells you they don't want to go there, so don't go there. Just love on them, tip them well, and tell them when you're leaving, "God bless you." You'll still move them closer to Jesus.

Being loving and generous moves people closer to Jesus only when they know you're a Christian. If they don't know you're a Christian, nothing happens spiritually, and you missed a great opportunity. Too many Christians believe that being a good person is being a good witness. But the world is full of good people doing good things that have nothing to do with God. Doing good things can be addictive for all the wrong reasons, the chief of which is being seen as a good person rather than a Christ follower.

Connecting the dots is one of the fun parts of faith sharing. Look for ways to connect other people to God in every conversation without raising eyebrows, saying things like, "These are my friends from church," or "Thank You, Lord, for this beautiful day," or quoting something your pastor said, or saying, "God bless you," when you're leaving. It's like sport finding different ways to reference God.

It's especially amazing how God directs our steps to specific people through divine appointments. In the case of our out-of-town restaurant, God directed us to a specific restaurant and a specific table in that restaurant to meet a specific server with a huge need. When we asked if there was something we could pray about, she said, "Oh my, yes!"

Her best friend, Dan, a truck driver, was out of state when he received a call that his only daughter had been molested and found unconscious in the back of a truck. Then she died just twenty minutes after he got to her bedside in the hospital. Can you imagine the pain?

This is why sharing our faith according to Luke 12:12 is so

important: "For the Holy Spirit will teach you in that very hour what you ought to say" (NKJV). This takes us to an entirely different level with God. Every faith-sharing opportunity is an opportunity to have God literally speak through us. That takes all the pressure off us. It's the ultimate on-the-job training program! John 14:26 provides this great promise from God: "But the Helper, the Holy Spirit, whom the Father will send in My name, He will teach you all things, and bring to your remembrance all things that I said to you" (NKJV). It's unbelievable how God reminds you of life stories and scriptures you may not have thought about for years that are a perfect match to that person's need.

In this case, even though I never give out my cell number, the Holy Spirit nudged me to give her my full name and cell number to give to her friend. Dan called me the next morning as low as a human being can be. He immediately began explaining that he was not only a Christian but a car guy who had watched my *Car Crazy* television show for years, followed my ministry activities on social media, and even knew that we had lost our daughter three years earlier. And then he said, "Can you possibly imagine what went through my mind just now when I was told 'Barry Meguiar wants you to call him'?"

I immediately broke out laughing and said, "I don't need to say anything more. Now you already know God is with you and will guide you through this." And he said, "You know, you're right." We had a powerful time of talking and praying together, using what we had learned from our own daughter's passing. When I called him a few days later, he started laughing, saying, "Just seconds ago my wife and I were talking about how you said, 'Don't let anything rob you of your joy.'"

Knowing his daughter was in heaven, I explained that his grief would subside with the reality that despite how she died, she was now the happiest she'd ever been. There's no need to stay unhappy when she's happy. And I reminded him that their separation was only temporary.

It turned out anger was a serious impediment for Dan and his wife having their joy restored. In this case, it was anger toward the "friends" of his daughter who had abandoned her—and it was huge. A phrase came to me that "anger is a self-inflicted punishment for a mistake someone else made." I explained that her "friends" had made a deadly mistake that may destroy their lives, and possibly his, if he didn't forgive them. That's a whole other story. But my new truck driver friend outside Kansas City, whom I never would have met had I not asked our waitress if there was something we could pray for her about, is now praising God for His faithfulness. Even our server has returned to her walk with the Lord.

To my great surprise, Dan came to town recently with a load of cattle right when I was recording podcasts. So I did a fascinating podcast with Dan the truck driver, getting his side of this amazing story. Adding to and confirming God's planning, Dan explained that his friend (our server) only works one day a week. Then, being a slow day, several servers were sent home, making it more certain that we would get her. And that afternoon her twelve-year-old daughter returned home from school with a cross and 8:28 written on her arm with a felt-tip marker—after I had just been emphasizing Romans 8:28 to her. Sometimes God wants to make sure we know that He knows.

PUSHED TO THE LIMITS

I can speak of anger from personal experience because at one time it was overwhelming Karen and me. Anger, even so-called "righteous anger," will eat you alive, rob you of your joy, and keep you from any thoughts of sharing your faith. You see, anger is the opposite of faith. Ephesians 4:26–27 instructs us not to let the sun go down on our anger, lest it give the devil a foothold.

Pushed to the very limits of forgiveness, Karen and I were faced with the reality that there's no end to God's forgiveness. There's no way to escape the illustrations of turning the other cheek, going the extra mile, and forgiving people seventy times seven. Believe me, we tried hard and failed miserably. At our darkest moment on this issue, Karen and I surrendered and promised God that we were going to forgive an individual who had tried for years to destroy us and our family. It was literally one of those "Your will, not ours, Lord" experiences. In all honesty, we were in absolute turmoil when we made that promise to God. I liken it to going into warp speed in one of the space movies, where everything around you shakes violently until it turns to total calm. That's what happened to us. Just like that, God gave us calm.

It's unbelievable! We defeated anger at that moment for the rest of our lives. And now God is using this huge life lesson for us to minister to more people who are struggling with anger than we could ever imagine. One of those was my new truck driver friend. One of the many reasons God allows huge trials in our lives is to grow us so we can help others grow. It's called the ministry of the body of Christ where iron sharpens iron. When God led Karen and me through our wilderness experience, He was preparing us to minister to a truck driver in Missouri.

This is what the Great Commission is all about. All of us are surrounded by hurting people who have no idea that God loves them, wants to protect them, and wants them to spend eternity with Him. But, perhaps even more amazing, I'm the one who benefits most from every faith-sharing experience. Nothing compares with knowing God just used you to move someone closer to Him. He sets the appointments and gives you

THIS IS WHAT IT'S ALL ABOUT

the words, but you need to follow His nudge. That's when you'll enjoy all the blessings God has planned for you.

People often ask me why I'm always so happy. This is why! Every day is an adventure. This book is filled with personal, real-life stories like this. This is how God wants all of us to live our lives every day—living for His purpose to seek and save the lost and moving everyone, every day, closer to Jesus. And the joy that comes from following His lead is the fulfillment of God's promise in John 15:11: "These things I have spoken to you, that My joy may remain in you, and that your joy may be full" (NKJV). When you bear fruit, His joy will remain in you, and your joy will be full. If you want to have all of your days filled with joy, regardless of your circumstances, this is how you do it. And that's why I'm repeating this message over and over throughout this book.

If you're a car guy, you know you need to keep exercising old cars to keep them running. When a car's engine has been sitting and not running for a while, it's hard to start. It either stutters or doesn't fire until you get new plugs. The old ones have lost their spark. The same is true for Christians today who have put themselves in neutral. They sat idling until they ran out of gas, and now they've lost their spark. If that's where you are right now, it's time for a complete overhaul. The great news is that God is still in the restoration business for those who are lost—and for those who have lost their spark.

Are you ready to get your spark back?

SCRIPTURES FOR DEEPER REFLECTION

- **If you're following Christ, you will move everyone, every day, closer to Him:** Mark 1:17 (NASB)

- **No one gets mad when you tell them, "God loves you!"** John 13:35 (NKJV)

- **It's freedom to know God gives you the words to say:** Luke 12:12 (NKJV)

- **It's supernatural how God reminds you what you've been told to tell others:** John 14:26 (NKJV)

- **Anger allows Satan to separate you from God:** John 15:11 (NIV)

- **Bearing fruit (new Christians) fills your life with God's joy:** John 15:11 (NKJV)

CHAPTER 7

THE MOST IMPORTANT COMMANDMENT

ERE'S SOMETHING FOR you to ponder: How many of your friends and loved ones would be left behind if the rapture happened tomorrow? It's a serious question because the rapture could easily happen tomorrow. In fact, we're to live our lives as if it will happen tomorrow. And knowing that, how concerned are you for the salvation of your unsaved friends and loved ones?

Penn Jillette is a tremendous entertainer with one of the longest-running shows in Las Vegas: *Penn & Teller*. He's also an avowed atheist. In a YouTube video, he tells the story of a nicely dressed man who spoke to him at the end of one of his shows and gave him a pocket New Testament and Psalms. His response was one of the most compelling calls for faith sharing I've ever heard. He said, "If you believe that there's a heaven and hell and people could be going to hell, how much would you have to hate me to not tell me? How much do you have to hate somebody to believe that everlasting life is possible and not tell them that?"[1]

The obvious conclusion is how much do you have to hate your unsaved friends and loved ones to not tell them? At the very least, you're not worrying about where they'll spend eternity, which means you don't care. If you were them and ended up in hell, would you not be angry with your former "Christian" friends for not warning you about hell? They'll have all their thoughts, including that one, tormenting them forever. You can't save anyone, but it is your responsibility to warn them. Ezekiel 33:8 warns us about that. This is deadly serious.

Jesus put it another way, flipping it from a hate perspective to a love agenda. When asked by the religious leaders, "What's the most important commandment?" Jesus replied, "'Love the Lord your

God with all your heart and with all your soul and with all your mind.' This is the first and greatest commandment. And the second is like it: 'Love your neighbor as yourself'" (Matt. 22:37–39). *Love God with your whole heart, soul, and mind, and love your neighbor as yourself.* If you do this, you'll fulfill the entire law (Matt. 22:36–40).

This parallels God's admonishment in Revelation 2:1 connecting your first love (Christ) to your first work (telling people about Christ) and Romans 8:28 compelling you to *love God and live your life for God's purpose*—to seek and save the lost. This is one of the most consistent themes in Scripture and in this book. You see, when you love your neighbor as yourself, you're as concerned for their salvation as you are your own. That's when you automatically fulfill the commandments by your desire to do everything possible to move everyone, every day, closer to Jesus. That truth sets you free! Living rightly to fulfill God's purpose to seek and save the lost becomes the driving force of your life and the most fun part of your day. And guess what? You're fulfilling all Ten Commandments without even thinking about it.

Of even greater importance is the impact "love your neighbor as yourself" has on you. The moment you understand that everything you say and do is moving everyone watching you closer or further away from God, it automatically changes everything you say and do—including any language, habit, or indulgence that's not honoring God and helping you lead people to Him. This is where the fulfillment of God's law in your life is made easy by your excitement for leading people to Jesus. Obligation is replaced with pure joy when people are being drawn to Him by everything you say and do.

One of my best "soul-winning machine" friends was on drugs and trafficked as a young girl. Most people don't get to where Christine is now from where she was then. Now she's a gleaming example of God's redeeming love. And she often tells me as a prolific soul-winner that there is no high in drug addiction that matches the high of leading someone to Jesus Christ, nor is there anything more addictive.

How many souls have been lost because of your failure to do what God tells you is your Great Commission: "Go ye therefore, and teach all nations, baptizing them in the name of the Father, and of the Son, and of the Holy Ghost" (Matt. 28:19, KJV)? Notice He doesn't say to go into the world and read your Bible or pray or be a good person. Nor does He say go ye, all who are gifted, trained, or paid. No! All of us have been sent, and He's holding all of us accountable.

I LET GOD DOWN

One of my famous car guy friends came down with a rare form of cancer when he was in his fifties. Like many of my car guy friends, he was a great guy but far from the Lord and without Christian friends living near him who could mentor him. I knew immediately that I needed to talk to Chip about the Lord. God was telling me, "Go ye," but it wasn't convenient. I was on the West Coast, he was on the East, and I was busy with my business, speaking engagements, a television show, and my ministry.

His condition declined rapidly over just a few months, and I knew even more I needed to get to him. God kept giving me the nudge. And then I got the call from his assistant while I was at the Amelia Island Concours in Florida that Chip had passed, and I wept out of grief and guilt.

I sat in my hotel room crying, "I let You down, God. I let Chip down." And there was nothing I could do about it. I couldn't get over the thought that Chip was going to spend eternity in hell because I was too busy to talk to him when he was alive. It was devastating. I loved Chip. He was my friend!

On the day of his service, they had his closest car guy friends get into an antique bus at the fairgrounds and drive to the church, where the parking lot was filled with cool cars. When I mentioned God to the guy sitting next to me on the bus, he said, "Well, Chip didn't have anything to do with God," and my stomach cramped. I was a mess.

Toward the end of the service, the young pastor quickly

acknowledged that all of us knew Chip better than he did. But then he continued by saying, "I didn't meet Chip until he became ill. But then we became close friends, and I led him to the Lord. And now he's in heaven." That's when I lost it altogether with the extreme emotions of joy and guilt.

I told God, "You saved my bacon this time. You saved Chip, and You saved me! But I promise You, I won't let You down again." And now when someone is dying that I can influence, I run to them. Because of Chip, there are several more people in heaven today because I've been there in time to lead them to Jesus at the end of their lives.

There's an added lesson to be learned from this real-life experience. I didn't fail to talk to Chip because I hated him. I loved Chip! But I wasn't loving him as myself. I wasn't as concerned for his salvation as I was my own. Otherwise, I would have been on the next plane.

If you have unsaved friends that you've been wimping out on, please learn from this mistake. God is "salvationing" us when He's loving us, and God has commissioned you to "salvation" everyone under your influence. More correctly, He wants to "salvation" everyone under your influence through you! You may be God's only point of contact with them.

Do you understand the importance of what I'm saying and what

**LOVING IS
SALVATIONING**

He's commanding? Sharing your faith is not a minor issue. It is *the* issue. It's the sum total, the end result. The entire purpose of God's love being poured out on you is to "salvation" you and to "salvation" everyone around you through you. With that understanding, listen to what John 13:34–35 says: "A new command I give you: [salvation] one another. As I have [salvationed] you, so you must [salvation] one another. By this everyone will know that you are my disciples, if you [salvation] one another." In layman's terms, this passage is saying you have no greater task or reason for being than to move everyone, every day, closer to Jesus.

Jerry Root and Stan Guthrie say it well in their book *The Sacrament of Evangelism*. They explain that every time we have an opportunity to share our faith with someone new, God's already there and has always been there, drawing that person to Himself. And when those seemingly spontaneous moments occur, they're actually divine appointments orchestrated by God. God literally invites you into His relationship with people, at the right moment, to be a physical manifestation of His loving on them. Think of the honor, privilege, and responsibility God is giving you at those moments. Here's a serious question: How often do you miss these opportunities by failing to follow God's nudge?

Here's another important fact: *God's Word never returns void* (Isa. 55:11). No matter what their reaction, their minds will never let them forget the truth of God's Word. Renowned brain surgeon and former presidential candidate Ben Carson explains that the brain never forgets anything it hears. Even in rejection, people will remember what you said and how you said it. And they'll know they can return to it when they're ready.

Again, Jesus said, "If you love me, keep my commands" (John 14:15). And the two great commandments are loving Him and loving your neighbors as yourself. There's no way around this overwhelming, comprehensive fact. Who can understand the outrageousness of God, the One who has the power to speak the universe into being, who has no beginning and no end, loving you as much as He loves His own Son—and trusting you as His ambassador to bring people to Him?

He's literally depending on you and me to lead people to Him. It's beyond comprehension!

SCRIPTURES FOR DEEPER REFLECTION

- **God expects all of us to move everyone, every day, closer to Jesus:** Ezekiel 33:8 (NKJV)

- **Never let anyone or anything come between you and God:** Matthew 22:37–38 (NIV)

- **God calls Christians to repent when their love for Him and sharing Him dies:** Revelation 2:1–5 (NKJV)

- **Loving God and living for His purpose is what life is all about:** Romans 8:28 (NKJV)

- **The Great Commission doesn't call us to study and pray or be "good":** Matthew 28:19 (KJV)

- **God has commanded us to love one another, without exception:** John 13:34–35 (NIV)

- **Every time you share God's Word, people are moved closer to Jesus:** Isaiah 55:11 (NKJV)

- **We prove to God we love Him by keeping His commandments:** John 14:15 (NIV)

CHAPTER 8

LIVING FOR GOD'S PURPOSE

ROMANS 8:28 WILL be the most referenced Bible verse in this book. You'll find it in the middle of this chapter and every chapter because of its importance and how poorly it's understood. It may be the second most important scripture in the Bible after John 3:16. Once you're a Christian, what could be more important than having everything work for good—from now until you get to heaven?

A pervasive thought in the church today is people's search for God's purpose for their lives. In a recent Bible study, I listened to a high-powered businessman, just retired, explain how he was now searching for God's purpose for his life. And there was group prayer asking God to help him find it. How poorly we read and understand the truth of God's Word.

There's not one word in the Bible that suggests God has a different purpose for each one of our lives. In fact, if God had one purpose for you and another for me and another for Himself, we would be at cross purposes. Romans 8:28 calls us to love Him and live for His purpose, not ours.

ONE PURPOSE

There's but one purpose for our lives, and it's God's purpose: to seek and save the lost—to move everyone, every day, closer to Jesus. If you're a Christian, the only thing that will matter a hundred years from now will be how many people are in heaven because of your influence.

I love my business, and I have dedicated my life to it. But it's not going to matter how many bottles of car wax I sold when I get to heaven. Nor is anything you did to gain fame or fortune or respect.

The only thing of value you can bring to heaven is souls. What could possibly match the knowledge that another human being is spending eternity in heaven because of your influence? That's a celebration that will never end!

Just as God's gift of eternal life is dependent on our accepting Jesus Christ as our Lord and Savior, God's promise to make everything work for good is dependent on your loving Him and living for His purpose. The exact wording is important: "to those who love God, to those who are the called according to His purpose" (Rom. 8:28, NKJV). Notice it doesn't say *and* to those who live for His purpose. If you do the one (love God), you'll do the other (live according to His purpose)!

When asked which is the most important commandment, Jesus tied loving Him and loving our neighbors as ourselves together. When we love our neighbors as ourselves, we're as concerned for their salvation as we are our own—living for His purpose to seek and save the lost. In His letter to the church at Ephesus, God tells Christians to repent for leaving their first love (Him) and no longer doing the first work of telling people about Jesus (Rev. 2:4–5). God is abundantly clear on what He expects us to do with our lives.

This theme runs consistently through the Bible from Genesis to Revelation. Being "called according to His purpose" is the clarion call for what we're to do with our lives: "for the Son of Man has come to seek and to save that which was lost" (Luke 19:10, NKJV). One of the great mysteries and truths of all time is that God reaches the lost through us. We get to share in this most glorious, righteous, and eternal task!

Listen to what 2 Corinthians 5:18 has to say: "Now all things are of God, who has reconciled us to Himself through Jesus Christ, and has given us the ministry of reconciliation" (NKJV). God couldn't make it any clearer: "Now then, we are ambassadors for Christ, as though God were pleading through us" (v. 20, NKJV).

It's true. The Spirit of Christ is inside of us and pleads to the world through us. God devised a plan wherein each one of us has our own unique role to play out His purpose in our lives. I can't help but think of that businessman who, after being the CEO of a huge company with huge influence, is only now trying to figure out how God wants to use him. He missed his opportunity when he had influence over thousands of employees.

If God is your first love and you're already trusting Him with your whole heart, look around you. You're already in the middle of your mission field. If you're in a secular environment, more than 73 percent of all the people you see are likely lost and in desperate need of what you have: "the peace of God, which surpasses all understanding" (Phil. 4:7, NKJV).

It's also true that Romans 8:28 is a stumbling block for those who only read the first part of that verse and say, "Everything will work for good." They miss the loving God part and living their lives for His purpose altogether. Millions of Christians believe everything should work for their good simply because they're Christians. Then they lose faith in God when things don't work according to what they perceive as good. Obviously, this is a total contradiction of Scripture, but it's a huge birthplace for loss of faith and bitterness toward God.

When you're a pastor, there's nothing better than knowing your people are repeating your message all week to their unsaved friends. And Romans 8:28 gives them all the incentive they need to do that. You can first remind them of Ephesians 4:11, which explains your mandate to equip them for ministry. And at the end of every sermon, you can remind them before they go out the door that everything in their life will work for good this week when they show God they love Him by keeping His commandments and living for His purpose by moving everyone, every day, closer to Jesus.

Who will not listen when you tell them God will make everything work for good if they do two things? And who wouldn't want to know what those two things are? And who wouldn't want to do those two things and enjoy living in God's promise to make everything in their lives work for good? This is one of the most powerful yet most ignored messages in our pulpits today.

WHAT IS GOOD?

The big question is, What does God view as good? And when will we see the good? Do you still have faith when you don't see the good? I heard a great quote today from a dear friend: "Sometimes faith will make you look stupid, until it starts to rain." It was almost one hundred years from when Noah first started building the ark to when the rain began. Can you imagine the abuse and mockery Noah experienced for a hundred years while his faith drove him to build the ark—which was more than good when it started to rain!

I'm a third-generation Southern California car guy, beach bum to the core, and God lover who was living on the same beach property my granddad purchased in 1942. I spent my earliest years on that property and caught my first fish off that pier when I was eight years old. At breakfast, my granddad would have us all get down on our knees to pray before we ate. The property was sold when he died in 1950. On one of our first dates, I showed Karen where my granddad's house once stood and told her about my memories. For our entire marriage our hearts' desire was to one day live on that property.

My life is poignant with the memories of my granddad on that property. And then it happened, and God granted the desires of our hearts with that property. We quoted Psalm 37:4 to everyone: "Delight yourself in the LORD, and He will give you the desires of your heart" (MEV). It was obvious to everyone: God had given us our final home to live out our lives, and we used it for one ministry event after another. It was so wonderful.

We were in total peace until God told us to move. "Say what? You gotta be kidding, Lord!" Without anyone knowing, we wept through a month of Christmas parties at our house. At our age, people don't move to a different state, away from their friends and family. And I'm a sun-seeking beach bum, living at the beach with all my toys. Come January, Karen and I sat facing each other, knowing what God was saying to both of us, and we said out loud, "Not our will but Yours be done." And we held each other and wept. A lifetime of following God's lead doesn't stop when you're eighty years old.

We sold our house in one day and bought a house in Arizona in one day. And now, a few years later, we realize He made us lie down in a green pasture. The ministry events we have now dwarf those we held in our small beach house; we've retained all our friends and have a host of new ones, and our ministry has exploded. We feel like we're newlyweds, just starting out with a new home and new friends and a new church on top of everything we already had. This is what happens when you trust God with wholehearted faith.

This is such an important point! Your view of good may not be God's view of good. His thoughts are not our thoughts.

Case in point: Mrs. Damato was one of the godliest women I've ever known, an incredible wife and mother who moved everyone closer to Jesus. But she suffered unrelenting pain from cancer in her final months of life. They moved her to the hospital for a prolonged period, where they still couldn't control the pain—and she died.

Thank God for His patience with me. I went to Mrs. Damato's funeral with anger toward Him. How could He let this precious woman suffer so much for no reason? This was a life lesson for me, and I hope for you too. During her funeral, three nurses took turns telling their version of the same story. Each one explained how they had no interest in God until they met Mrs. Damato. They were struck by her joy and peace in the midst of her pain. Each of them explained how they encountered God through Mrs. Damato and committed their lives to Jesus Christ because of her. One of them said she heard Mrs. Damato singing praises to God as she walked past her room on the day she died. Mrs. Damato lived for God's purpose to her very last breath—and her faith never wavered.

Notice that Romans 8:28 doesn't say things will work together for your good. It just says "all things work together for good." And the good that God orchestrates is always redemptive, bringing more people to Him. Knowing those three nurses accepted the Lord, do you think Mrs. Damato was upset with God for allowing her to have the pain? I think not! Knowing all the people who accepted the Lord because of our daughter Nicole's passing, do you think we're upset? I think not! And great is her reward. (See Matthew 5:12.)

It's a bit like birth pains. And in this case, we're talking pain orchestrated by God for His purpose. When we trust God, our focus eventually moves from the pain of the birth to something new and wonderful. And with the temporariness of our time on earth, through God's eyes, we may not know His reason for our pain until we get to heaven. Romans 8:18 tells us: "For I consider that the sufferings of this present time are not worthy to be compared with the glory which shall be revealed in us."

Living for God's purpose is eternal!

SCRIPTURES FOR DEEPER REFLECTION

- **We're called to live for God's purpose, not our purpose:** Romans 8:28 (NKJV)

- **When we stop doing the first work (sharing our faith), our love for God grows cold:** Revelation 2:1–5 (NKJV)

- **God's sole purpose for coming to earth was the redemption of mankind:** Luke 19:10 (NKJV)

- **Jesus transferred to us the responsibility of bringing people to Him:** 2 Corinthians 5:18–20 (NKJV)

- **The world is desperate for the peace that comes from God:** Philippians 4:7 (NKJV)

- **A role of the pastor is to equip us for ministry:** Ephesians 4:11–12 (ESV)

- **God knows better than us how to fulfill the desires of our heart:** Psalm 37:4 (MEV)

- **Far better to have eternal rewards in heaven than temporary rewards on earth:** Matthew 5:12 (NIV)

- **Our current suffering will be forgotten forever when we see Jesus:** Romans 8:18 (ESV)

CHAPTER 9

LIVING IN THE SWEET SPOT

KAREN AND I have been to the historic sites of all seven churches in the Book of Revelation that received letters, or really personal messages from God. We sat with the foremost New Testament scholars of the Assemblies of God and soaked in every word they had to say.

All of the letters relate to what we're seeing in the church today. But the letter to the church at Ephesus seems to be the most on-target. In my words, God says, "I know you're faithful in attendance and sacrifice, and you know good teaching from bad. But I have this against you: you've left Me as your first love, and you're no longer telling people about Me, which is the first work, the first thing you did when you received Me." (See Revelation 2:1–4.)

And—remembering that He's speaking to us, the church—He calls us to repent! He calls us to return to our first love (Him) and to doing the first work of sharing our faith or He'll remove our candlestick (our testimony). And that's exactly what has happened. With so few of us still doing the first work, the testimony of the church is almost nonexistent. We're seeing that verse, that promise, manifest at this very moment in America.

When a new believer prays the sinner's prayer and accepts Jesus Christ as their Lord and Savior, there's no question who they would describe as their first love. God just forgave them of all their sins, saved them from going to hell, and gifted them with eternal life in heaven. Escaping the guilt and penalty of their sins, being brought into the family of God, and reigning with Him forever over the angels will wholly implant God in your psyche as your first love.

That's why the first thing, the first work, every new believer does is to tell everyone about Jesus—"I was blind, and now I see!" You can't stop a new Christian from sharing their faith because God is their first love. The two are inseparable! That's why the degree to which you share your faith is the barometer of your relationship with God. Are you going through the motions of being a Christian or the emotions of loving God with your whole heart? If you're no longer sharing your faith, chances are God is no longer your first love. I understand that this might be a shock to you. You may be thinking, "How could this possibly be? Of course God is my first love." But is He?

Here's an easier way to look at it. We naturally talk about the things we love and things that excite us most. If you had a great burger last night, chances are you're telling people about it today. If your team just won the championship, you're probably talking about it nonstop to everyone who will listen. Do you get my drift?

When you first got saved, your excitement for God filled your life. He was top-of-mind and in most of your conversations. But life is filled with lots of things that grab our attention and excitement and compete with God's first position in our lives. It happens without you even realizing it. And over time, over years, it's easy for God to not stay top-of-mind—unless your focus stays fixed on moving everyone, every day, closer to Jesus. That's exactly why sharing your faith is so important.

In Matthew 5:13–14, we're called to be salt and light. Most of us have heard countless sermons on the efficacy of salt and light. But there's only one characteristic salt and light have in common. They both change their environment. I'll go into more detail on this later, but we're failing big-time to change our environment.

Here's the message of this book in simple terms. You need to follow this closely: When God is your first love, you'll do the first work. And when you do the first work, God will remain your first love. This speaks to the very core of why God wants the sharing of your faith to be your highest priority. It's how God keeps you on your knees, in the Word, and ignited.

Discipleship programs remind us of what we already know. We need to be on our knees and in the Word every day. We know that.

But our days are long and busy and tiring, and then there's the evening agenda. It's way too easy to rationalize why we don't have time to read and pray tonight, night after night—unless you're an ignited faith sharer.

But when you're sharing your faith, no one has to tell you to study your Bible and be on your knees. In fact, nothing can stop you from praying for people you witnessed to that day and searching for the answers you need by tomorrow morning. This is when the fun begins and your faith explodes as God leads you to the right scriptures. Proverbs 2:3–4 describes the excitement: "Call out for insight and cry aloud for understanding...look for it as for silver and search for it as for hidden treasure." And in the process, you're the one who grows the most!

WE ALREADY KNOW THAT

Every Christian knows they should be in the Word and on their knees every day. The problem is doing it. But that's not a problem when you're focused on moving everyone, every day, closer to Jesus. And here's the best part: the more you do it, the more you love doing it, as it explodes your faith and changes lives every day. Loving God above all else permeates everything you do and say with joy. And it keeps getting better and better.

I'm not an anomaly. We tend to attract people to us who are like us. And I'm finding people everywhere who are as much or more excited than I am about being "first love" Christians who are living for His purpose. This is not about me. It's about God's promise to all of us who hold Him as our first love and live our lives for Him. Granted, we all have different types of personalities, but He fills everyone with joy who simply does what He's called us to do.

You also have choices! First-love Christians always have an abundance of good things being offered to them. But they're not all the same. God didn't tell you to go into the world and be a good person or do good things or even to read your Bible and pray. The Great Commission (Matt. 28:19–20) makes it abundantly clear that your number one responsibility is to tell people about Jesus.

There are so many wonderful programs for things like feeding and clothing the poor around the world that are honorable. But if they're not sharing the message of salvation at the same time, they're merely helping people be better dressed and better fed on their way to hell. We're called to be good stewards of our time and resources. There must be ROI, a return on our investment in souls, for everything that we do and support. Otherwise, we're not being good stewards of the resources God has placed in our hands. God is holding us responsible, not only for being good givers, but for the return on our investments in souls.

It's interesting how easily good things, even ministries, can take first position in our lives. It's not that they're wrong necessarily. It's where they fall in the list of our priorities. One of our radio ministry partners shared with me how his faith was being shaken by an attack on a side ministry he had birthed that was beginning to flourish. A few questions revealed how this ministry had become his focus over everything else. In fact, its troubles were diminishing his love for and trust in God. It wasn't that the ministry was bad or not something God wanted to bless; the problem was simply the priority he had given it. You may be in that situation right now. Because this was a godly man, he understood exactly what I was saying and made an immediate course adjustment, restoring God to His first love position.

WHO'S YOUR GOD?

Most family businesses have family issues that are not easily solved. Because half of our family members were completely opposed to being in the retail market, our board meetings were not uneventful. Several times it seemed impossible for us to continue in business together. At one point I actually called a meeting to bring attention to the fact that the only thing we could agree on was that we couldn't agree on anything. And this was happening in the midst of blinding growth. They simply couldn't understand it, and the numbers scared them.

This sent me on a two-and-a-half-year search for someone to

help us as a counselor or partner or purchaser. I prayed harder during that period of time than ever before in my life. It seemed like every day God would ask me, "Do you trust Me now?" And I would answer yes, thinking it would come to an end the next day. But the days led to months and then to years. It's important to point out that I never lost my faith that God was going to solve our problems. I knew that!

After two and a half years, I was listening on my car radio to a preacher I didn't know who was asking, "Who's your God?" I immediately thought, "At least I have that question under control." Then he asked the question again: "Who's your God?" At that point, I reached over to change the station, but before I did he said, "Whatever fills your prayers is your God." It was like he shot a bullet into my forehead. It was a *rhema* word—a message directly from God.

For two and a half years I had been praying nonstop for my business, asking God for His help in finding the right person, getting the right appointments, having my phone calls answered, and solving my problem. I had made my business my god. I couldn't believe it! How could I do that? I knew better. I couldn't wait to get home on my knees and beg God for forgiveness. I was so ashamed. I told God He could take my business and everything else. All I wanted was intimacy with Him, closeness with Him, to honor Him with every ounce of my being. This was a turning point in my life. And this has been my prayer ever since. I've made sure to never make that mistake again. God is and will always be my first love.

It was more than ten years before I allowed myself to ask for anything related to our business again. Here's the humorous part: within two weeks of that experience, the family reconciled, my uncle had a heart attack, and I found myself by his side praying for him. I could have shortened that two-and-a-half-year period by two and a half years if I had only kept God in His rightful position of being the first love of my life. God wanted to bless my business, but He wouldn't do it as long as I made my business my god. Are you hearing me?

The late Andraé Crouch had a wonderful song called "Take Me Back." In it, he asks God to take him back to the place where he first believed. That song is so powerful because God is always our first love at the moment of our salvation. And the moment we make anything else our first love, our automatic knee-jerk to do the first work ends.

After Jesus told Peter to cast his net on the other side of his boat, he caught the biggest catch of his life. But he didn't glory in the catch. He ran to Jesus, who asked him, "Do you love Me more than these [more than your livelihood, your life]?" And Peter said, "Yes, Lord, You know that I love You," to which Jesus replied, "Then feed My sheep." (See John 21:15–17.) Jesus asked Peter the same question three times. Each time Peter said yes, and each time Jesus replied, "Then feed My sheep."

How about you? Do you love God? Then feed His sheep!

My daily prayer is to not let anything separate me from God's love. As long as I stay in that sweet spot, I'm sensitive to the fact that He's loving people and drawing people to Him through me. Psalm 139:23–24 says it well: "Search me O God and know my heart; test me and know my anxious thoughts. See if there is any offensive way in me, and lead me in the way everlasting."

So here's the formula: first love = first work = first love = first work!

SCRIPTURES FOR DEEPER REFLECTION

- **The church today has largely lost its focus and its lampstand (testimony):** Revelation 2:1–4 (NKJV)

- **The "saltiness" (testimony) of the church is being trampled under the foot of man:** Matthew 5:13–14 (NLT)

- **This is where the adventure begins:** Proverbs 2:3–5 (NIV)

- **Your number-one responsibility is to tell people about Jesus:** Matthew 28:19–20 (NIV)

- **When we love God, we'll feed His sheep (share our faith):** John 21:15–17 (NKJV)

- **Pure transparency with God brings pure joy:** Psalm 139:23–24 (KJV)

CHAPTER 10

YOU HAVE A PULPIT

MOST PEOPLE WOULD never guess I used to be an introvert. Karen, who's never known a stranger, was my gift from God. Whenever we were in large crowds, I literally hid behind her until she broke the ice and I felt comfortable to join the conversation.

I get a kick out of people who say, "Well, if I had your personality, I'd be sharing my faith." Somehow I missed the "go ye into the world if you have the right personality" part. I learned to share my faith despite being an introvert. Sharing my faith led me out of being an introvert.

By 1976 I had transitioned from agonizingly sharing my faith on rare occasions to always being ready and excited for the next opportunity. It was as if God was sending more people to me now that He knew He could count on me. Every encounter was bringing me more joy and more confidence—exactly as the Scriptures promise—to the point I felt God was leading me into full-time ministry.

I remember the exact encounter that put me over the edge. I had just finished a sales call with a retail chain in New Jersey. It was cold and snowing, and I couldn't wait to get in my car and turn the heater on. I was with my Jewish manufacturer's rep, who represented me in New York/New Jersey and had made the appointment that we'd just left. And he said, "Before you put the car in gear, would you pray for me?" It was completely out of the blue.

I call it chumming for the Lord. We're called to be fishers of men. When you deep-sea fish, you throw out small fish called chum to catch the big fish. From the back of the boat, while you're trolling slowly, you throw out one small fish after another to create a "chum line." At any given time, I have spiritual chum lines going out in every direction.

If the marlin isn't hungry, he keeps right on swimming. Oh, but if he's hungry, he makes his way up the chum line consuming each progressive fish until he bites my hook. There's only one thing more beautiful than seeing a marlin coming up my chum line! It's seeing a hungry, lost soul coming up my spiritual chum line.

Here's how you do it. Always, always watch for where you can insert God into a conversation without raising eyebrows. It's like sport, and it keeps you on your toes spiritually. You can spontaneously thank God for the beautiful day or repeat a joke that your pastor said on Sunday or talk about one of your friends from church. It's not about a spiritual message. It's about letting everyone know, without making it an issue, that you're a Christian.

Here's the great added benefit: all of us need extra incentive to live our lives for Christ out loud. It can be tiring being good for the sake of being good and reading our Bibles and praying out of obligation, without purpose. Doing it simply for the sake of doing it is religious and deadly. Ah, but doing it knowing you're in the game, God is using you, and people are being drawn to God because of you brings purpose to everything you do. This is why loving God and loving your neighbor as yourself completes the entire law; you're doing all the right things for the right reasons. It's fun!

In this case, my Jewish rep was in crisis and believed I could help him because of my faith. We'd never had an outright spiritual conversation up to that moment, but he knew I knew God because I'd been throwing out chum. You don't have to be on a soapbox to communicate your love for God. You simply live it, with every ounce of your being, in preparation for making a clear presentation of the hope that's within you (1 Pet. 3:15). I never push, and I never argue. I simply let people know I'm a Christian and available to them.

One of the great lies of the church is that "actions speak louder than words." They do not! "Faith comes from what is heard, and what is heard comes through the message about Christ" (Rom. 10:17, csb). Actions speak *before* our words. If our actions match our words, our words have power, regardless of how poorly we say them. If our

ONE OF THE CHURCH'S GREAT LIES

actions fail to match our words, our words are powerless, regardless of how eloquent they might sound. When you walk the talk, people pay attention to your talk.

With chumming comes responsibility. Now that they know you're a Christian, you're a city set on a hill that cannot be hidden (Matt. 5:14). From that point on, everything you do and say is leading that person closer or further away from God. For me, this is the best part: knowing that everything I do and say is leading people to Him. That's all the incentive I need to live the life God wants me to live.

It's no longer about blindly doing the right things and worrying about doing the wrong things. It's about living every moment of your life as His representative—His ambassador—to the 80 percent of the people around you who have no idea that God loves them and wants them to spend eternity with Him. They are your mission field.

After I returned home from that business trip, I found it hard to concentrate on my work. I kept thinking about my Jewish rep and how easy and fun it was to share my faith with him. Finally, in desperation, I closed the door to my office and prayed the most fervent prayer of my life.

I told God that I felt He was leading me into full-time ministry, and I was all-in if that's what He wanted me to do. I loved my business, and it was on the move, so I had to know for sure God wanted me to leave it. It was a huge decision for me. I told Him what He already knew: I had two little girls to feed, and our family business would probably fail without me as the third-generation leader. We were doing about a million dollars in gross sales at the time.

To cap it off, I said these exact words: "You're almost going to have to speak to me in an audible voice for me to make this radical change in my life. But once I know, I'll never look back." I was ready to give up my passion and dreams for my business to go wherever God wanted me to go. Most importantly, He knew that!

Twenty minutes later Dave McNutt walked into my office. Even though Dave went to my church, we had never talked or even exchanged a glance, and here he was in my office. He explained that he was in the area and thought he should stop in and ask, "How's it going?"

Knowing that he'd grown up as an MK (missionary kid) in Africa, I made a snap decision that he wasn't interested in cool cars and shiny paint finishes. So I began telling Dave some of my faith-sharing adventures, leading to my most recent experience with the Jewish rep. That's when he leaned forward in excitement and said, "God's given you a wonderful ministry here, hasn't He?"

I couldn't believe what he'd just said, and I asked him why he said it. He replied that pastors can't reach the people I was reaching as a businessman. Then he concluded with this amazing statement: "It's obvious that your business is your pulpit." Now I knew my business and ministry overlapped, but it was an entirely new thought that they were one and the same.

I was in shock at that point. I quickly told him what I had just prayed to God about, and he said, "That explains it!" When I asked what he meant by that, he said he had just dropped missionaries off at the Orange County airport and was driving up Red Hill, the closest main street to my office, when God told him to go see Barry Meguiar. He immediately told God, "I don't know anything about Barry Meguiar, I have no idea what kind of business he's in, and I'll make a fool of myself." But God didn't stop until he entered my office.

This is also a lesson in obedience. If Dave had not been obedient to God's nudge, I would have been a horrible pastor. I'm a businessman. That was 1976, and now, over forty years later, my business is still my pulpit.

It's so easy to pray and ask God about what He wants you to do in the future. But wherever you are right now, that's your pulpit. And it's your responsibility to use it, in every way possible, to move everyone you influence closer to Jesus. "As each one has received a gift," wrote the apostle Peter, "minister it to one another, as good stewards of the manifold grace of God" (1 Pet. 4:10, NKJV).

Scotland's Eric Liddell, who won a Gold Medal at the 1924

Olympics, saw running as his pulpit and used it to point people to Jesus. He said, "God made me fast. And when I run, I feel His pleasure."[1] The movie *Chariots of Fire* is based on his life.

It's so easy to compartmentalize our lives into categories like work and church and only encounter God on Sundays. But when you are a "first love" Christian, nothing is secular. Your life is one grand opportunity to represent God to those who are lost, wherever you find them, be it in a waiting room, on the phone with an operator, in line at Starbucks, or even sitting next to you in church. The supermarket can be just as sacred as your sanctuary. You're in full-time ministry!

ALWAYS BE READY

Karen and I went to one of our favorite restaurants in Beverly Hills with dear friends for a great evening, having no idea what was about to happen. After I took a picture of everyone around the table, a very handsome, tall, Black gentleman wearing a hoodie asked if I would like him to take a picture of us with me in it. Of course, I said yes, and he took special care to make sure the picture was perfect.

After he took the picture, we bantered and exchanged names. He told us he was in the music business. After he left our table, we googled him and discovered that he's a famous rapper. When he asked what I do for a living, I explained that I make car wax. He was not impressed but very nice, and he returned to his table.

A few minutes later, one of my guests, Valerie, handed me a bottle of our Ultimate Quik Detailer and told me to go give it to him. Valerie had called her driver in her Bentley sitting out front and asked him to get a bottle from her trunk and bring it to her. I pushed back saying that would be embarrassing. But she insisted, and I obediently did as she asked.

I went over to his table where he was having dinner with three of his female assistants and explained how my friend had retrieved a bottle of our car wax from her Bentley that was sitting beside his Bentley out in front, and she insisted that I give it to him. And he said, "Oh, you mean Valerie." He remembered her name! He immediately recognized the package and wanted to know the story behind it. So I explained that it was that "white privilege" thing, working eighteen-hour days for thirty years following God's lead—and he burst out laughing.

Now, mind you, I would not have said that unless I knew it would make him laugh. The Holy Spirit had already given us that kind of relationship where we could laugh at ourselves and be real. Then he poured out his heart, saying that his values matched my values. The Lord prompted me to ask if he expressed those values in his music—and he didn't know what to say.

I asked him if we could pray about that, and he and his three female assistants immediately stretched their hands out to hold hands, and I prayed. I thanked God for the privilege of meeting this amazing, handsome, exceedingly talented guy and for the favor God had given him to influence a generation. When I finished, he gave me his cell number and asked me if we could spend more time together.

"The steps of a good man are ordered by the LORD: and he delighteth in his way" (Ps. 37:23, KJV). And God directs the steps of those in search of Him as well. Think about it: on that particular night, God directed both of us to the same restaurant in Beverly Hills at the very same time, more than an hour's drive away from both of us, so that a famous rapper and a guy who peddles car wax could have a God-focused conversation.

Let me add, you really can't prepare yourself for spontaneous faith-sharing conversations. For the most part you have no idea when they will happen or where the conversations will take you. That's why I find comfort in Luke 12:12: "For the Holy Spirit will teach you at that time what you should say." Mark 13:11 says it even better: "Don't worry in advance about what to say. Just say what God tells you at that time, for it is not you who will be speaking, but the Holy Spirit" (NLT).

Some of the biggest excuses for not sharing your faith are, "I don't know enough," "I'm not qualified," and "That's not my gift."

But that's all they are, excuses. God does all the work! He makes the appointments, and He gives you the words to say. All you have to do is be on the ready, watching for every opportunity to move everyone, every day, closer to Jesus.

Wherever you are is your pulpit!

SCRIPTURES FOR DEEPER REFLECTION

- **Expect every conversation to be an opportunity to lead everyone closer to Jesus:** 1 Peter 3:15 (MEV)

- **Just being a "good person" doesn't lead anyone to Jesus:** Romans 10:17 (CSB)

- **A Christian today is watched and judged by everyone:** Matthew 5:14 (ESV)

- **Wherever you are right now, that's your pulpit:** 1 Peter 4:10 (NKJV)

- **It's a continual adventure when you allow God to direct your steps:** Psalm 37:23 (KJV)

- **Your faith explodes when God directs your steps and gives you the words to say:** Luke 12:12 (NIV)

- **There's zero prep time/zero stress when you share your faith God's way:** Mark 13:11 (NLT)

CHAPTER 11

SPIRITUAL ATROPHY

ATROPHY REFERS TO wasting away and deterioration, owing to lack of use and defective nutrition. Use it or lose it! Without proper attention, exercise, and nutrition, atrophy is unavoidable. Everything eventually and ultimately breaks down to nothingness.

On a personal basis I love atrophy. Because of atrophy, most surfaces need to be polished, waxed, and protected. It's wonderful! Without atrophy I'd be out of business. And here's the key: you can reverse atrophy or prevent it from happening altogether. There's a direct connection between this fact and your walk with God.

During a long hospital stay, after the doctors had given up on me, God worked a miracle and I walked out of the hospital—with a walker. I could hardly stand up. My lungs were shot, and my ability to walk was almost gone. I felt like I was eighty years old (that's a joke). It was a long road back, but I made it back, and now I'm better than ever. But I learned the hard lesson that when you don't use your muscle strength, it disappears quickly.

Now I understand that this is a stretch, and you can call it what you want, but I see spiritual atrophy running rampant in the church today. In fact, it could be what best describes the church today. We've stopped exercising our faith! As a result, the American church is the weakest it's been since America was founded as one nation under God, with liberty and justice for all.

Of all the reasons given for America's problems today, they could easily be ascribed to spiritual atrophy. Less than 30 percent of our population was still attending church regularly in 2019, pre-COVID.[1] In the 1700s, our founders understood the biggest threat to America would be what I'm now calling spiritual atrophy. When asked what form of government had been chosen for this new nation, Benjamin Franklin gave his famous quote: "A republic, if you can keep it."[2]

On October 11, 1798, John Adams went further by describing in detail the biggest threat to our nation's survival. Within his proclamation on that day, Adams said: "We have no government armed with power capable of contending with human passions unbridled by...morality and religion." Then he added: "Our Constitution was made only for a moral and religious people. It is wholly inadequate to the government of any other."[3]

Our founders would have understood far better than most of our political and church leaders today what is happening to America. And yes, I call it spiritual atrophy. The further we get away from God as a nation and as individuals, the more chaos and divisions we'll experience. And the closer we are to God as individuals and a nation, the more we'll enjoy peace and joy and love. The basis of our problems in America today is neither political nor racial. They're the result of spiritual atrophy.

HOW IS THIS POSSIBLE?

I often talk with people who have been Christians and faithful church attenders for decades who tell me they don't know enough to share their faith. How is this possible? They've listened to at least three hundred sermons a year for ten years. That's three thousand sermons' worth of information they've consumed and can't repeat. You know what I call that! If you don't use the truth of God's Word, you lose it. It's spiritual atrophy! That's the real reason sharing your faith is such a critical part of your life. You immediately start using what you're learning!

Most Christians can't even tell you what their pastor preached on the previous Sunday unless they've used it to move people closer to Jesus throughout the week. You have to use it if you want to keep it. Pastors, your sermons will have far greater impact on your people when you challenge them to use your sermons to share their faith. And that's how you impact your community. It's a win/win proposition.

Failing to grow spiritually births lukewarm believers who are hearers only of the Word. James 1:22–25 (NKJV) warns us of the consequences:

> But be doers of the word, and not hearers only, deceiving yourselves. For if anyone is a hearer of the word and not a doer, he is like a man observing his natural face in a mirror; for he observes himself, goes away, and immediately forgets what kind of man he was. But he who looks into the perfect law of liberty and continues in it, and is not a forgetful hearer but a doer of the work, this one will be blessed in what he does.

Then there's Revelation 3:16, which graphically describes God's reaction to lukewarm believers to the point of spewing them out of His mouth. It appears that nothing turns God's stomach like those who have "a form of godliness, but [deny] the power thereof" (2 Tim. 3:5, KJV). Christians have allowed spiritual atrophy to destroy their faith and their walk with the Lord.

I mentioned this before, but it bears repeating. Satan is using fear as his primary weapon against us today. Fear is paralyzing Christians, stopping them in their tracks and causing them to lose their faith. Over 80 percent of all Americans, including Christians, now report that they're living in fear, which is the opposite of faith. And without faith it's impossible to share your faith. You can't share what you don't have. Satan is sterilizing Christians with fear so we can't reproduce ourselves.

But you can't blame the entirety of spiritual atrophy on Satan. Much, if not most, of it is self-induced. Whether it's activities pulling you away from church or distractions pulling you away from God, you can only tread water for so long before you start to sink. And this is especially true now with the world in complete turmoil and Christians under full attack. Half-hearted, middle-of-the-road Christianity will not serve you well in the last days.

If you're not in a church where the Word is proclaimed and the Spirit is moving, your chance of avoiding atrophy in your life is almost zero. The fellowship of believers joining together in corporate worship, with scriptural truths being proclaimed, has never been more important. We're under attack, and there's nowhere else to run. Hebrews 10:25 warns us: "And let us not neglect our meeting together, as some people do, but encourage one another, especially now that the day of his return is drawing near" (NLT). God knew two thousand years ago what we would be going through today and what it's going to take for us to survive spiritually.

One of the most troubling and perplexing issues of our day is the apostasy that's dividing our churches, denominations, Christian universities, seminaries, and worst of all, our families. Even those who are not persuaded by false doctrines are having the wind taken out of their sails by the attack from within on biblical truths, which is a win for Satan. It's incredible! Christians are now afraid of sharing their faith for fear of offending other "Christians."

I'm at a loss to understand how people can depart from the truth of God's Word into doctrines that come from demons. First Timothy 4:1 describes it perfectly: "But the Spirit explicitly says that in later times some will fall away from the faith, paying attention to deceitful spirits and doctrines of demons" (NASB). This is a major prophecy coming to pass and proving that we're in the last days. Spiritual atrophy is very real!

Then there are those who can't blame anyone but themselves for their spiritual decline. Most Christians have followed the crowd into the spiritual purgatory of fear, avoiding the assembling of the saints, watching church services online, and now find themselves basically dead in the water.

Complacency is the biggest problem in the church today and the bottom-line reason America is falling apart at its seams. It's so easy to point fingers and express anger toward those who are causing the problems today. But for the most part they're not bad people. They're lost people who are not going to church and will never know there's a God who loves them unless we (Christians) tell them. But we're not telling them!

THE BIGGEST PROBLEM

Here's my best and most often stated statistic: over 80 percent of the unchurched know the world is out of control, would like to believe there's a God who can end the chaos, are looking for someone to tell them, and already have at least one Christian in their life that they trust. We could ignite America with revival in thirty days if we weren't languishing in spiritual atrophy. Let's put the pieces together. The church has atrophied, so Christians have atrophied, and America has atrophied into a spiritual abyss. The most important thing we can do for ourselves and the most patriotic thing we can do for America is to start moving everyone, every day, closer to Jesus. You can't change the world, but you can change *your* world. And if all of us change our worlds, we'll change the world!

Every time you follow God's nudge to move someone closer to Him, your own understanding of biblical truth increases, and your faith explodes. That's why Satan fights so hard to keep you from sharing your faith. One of his most successful weapons is the fear of being asked questions you can't answer. But that's when the fun begins. Just admit you don't have the answer. No one expects you to be a Bible scholar, and knowing every answer can actually be annoying. I know it's counterintuitive, but you actually build credibility by not being a know-it-all. Just ask if they will allow you to pray for them over the next few days in search of the answer in God's Word. They never say no, and God always provides you with the answer.

This is the antidote for spiritual atrophy, where reading your Bible and praying moves from being an obligation and a religious act to one of the most fun parts of your life. It's funny how this works. When you're sharing your faith, you can't get on your knees or into the Bible fast enough. At every opportunity you're asking for God's help to give you answers, scouring the Word and concordances and commentaries. It's like searching for treasure, adding purpose if not obsession to your Bible reading and prayer life. This is another game changer.

Proverbs 2:4–5, 7–8 tells us to search for truth in God's Word "as you would for silver, seek them like hidden treasures. Then you will understand what it means to fear the LORD, and you will gain knowledge of God....He grants a treasure of common sense to the honest. He's a shield to those who walk with integrity. He guards the paths of the just and protects those who are faithful to him" (NLT). This is how you can walk in faith with "joy unspeakable and full of glory" (1 Pet. 1:8, KJV), no matter how dark this world gets from now until you see Him face-to-face.

From the beginning of this chapter, I've told you that spiritual atrophy is not only reversible but can be prevented from happening altogether. Do you know why God is calling, mandating, commanding, and commissioning you to share your faith? It's obviously more than important. I suspect this will come as a shock to you, but it's secondarily to win the lost and primarily to win you!

The scripture that explains why God insists you share your faith is found in Isaiah 43:10. Listen to what it says: "'You are my witnesses,' declares the LORD, 'and my servant whom I have chosen, so that you may know and believe me and understand that I am [God].'" Notice He doesn't say so you will know more or believe more or understand more.

There is no other way by which you can experience the intimacy with God that comes from His speaking through you and changing the life of the person in front of you. There's a oneness with God in those moments that's indescribable. That's when you'll know and believe and understand that He is God—and you'll never again have spiritual atrophy.

SCRIPTURES FOR DEEPER REFLECTION

- **Most Christians have become hearers only, denying the power of God:** James 1:22–25 (NKJV)

- **God is not happy with Christians sitting on the bench and doing nothing:** Revelation 3:16 (NIV)

- **Pick your friends carefully, lest they pull you down:** 2 Timothy 3:5 (KJV)

- **There has never been a more important time to be with believers in church:** Hebrews 10:25 (NLT)

- **Apostasy in the church confirms we're in the last days:** 1 Timothy 4:1 (NASB)

- **Sharing your faith turns the obligation of Bible study into an adventure:** Proverbs 2:4–8 (NLT)

- **Faith is the substance of things hoped for, the evidence of things unseen:** 1 Peter 1:8 (KJV)

- **It's secondarily about winning the lost and primarily about igniting you:** Isaiah 43:10 (NIV)

CHAPTER 12

IT'S NOT A "YIKES!" IT'S A "WOW!"

JUST THE MENTION that God mandates you share your faith is enough to make most Christians say, "Yikes!" But it's actually a "Wow!" that makes this chapter one of the most fun to read.

Mind you, for me, it was fifty years ago when I said, "Yikes!" The journey was slow at first, and then it took off, and it's been a race to keep up with God ever since. And all the while, my life has been full to overflowing with the challenges and responsibilities of being a husband, dad, granddad, friend, businessman, board member, and church lay minister, and an active part of all the wonderful ministries God has placed on our hearts. We've been busy, Karen and I.

I started sharing my faith not because I wanted to but because I knew God wanted me to—and I did everything wrong. Karen was way better than me because she loves being with new people. I was an introvert, forced to be an extrovert by the sharing of my faith.

If you want to get a crowd to come to your church for a meeting on a weeknight, don't tell them it's an evangelism class. No one comes! We discovered that firsthand at two different churches. We're wired a bit different. The fact that we didn't want to do it is what compelled us to do it, for fear of disappointing God. Looking back, we're recipients of the promise found in Matthew 25:23 (NLT) of being given more important responsibilities (like writing this book) if we're faithful in the small things.

Our first experience came in 1966, knocking on doors at night in Detroit. You definitely wouldn't do that today, but we did, and that's how we cut our teeth in faith sharing, asking people if we could pray for them, and inviting them to our church. But even in our naivete, God blessed us and those who opened their doors to us.

We did the same thing for Santa Ana (Orange County) First Assembly in 1972. I remember so well walking up to those front doors hoping no one would be at home. It was one small step for mankind! Then came the structure and programs and points to memorize and Bibles highlighted with all the right verses to repeat in sequence and so much more.

Never having been a good student, I wasn't a good evangelism student, and I always had great problems staying with the script. Somewhere between point two and point three, the person I was sharing with would go off script to an entirely different subject, and I had to get them back on track so I could deliver point three. I found myself getting upset with them, upset with God, and upset with myself. It was not working for me.

There are times when scriptures you've read for years suddenly jump into your mind—often referred to as *rhema* in the Greek. That happened to me one day during my Bible study time. In distress over my faith-sharing debacles, I heard Jesus saying in John 13:35, "By this everyone will know that you are my disciples, if you love one another." I about jumped out of my skin! He wasn't saying they will know I'm His disciple by my memoriza-

A RHEMA WORD

tion of a script, but by my love. Well, I thought, I can do that! And I've been doing it ever since. I just love on people.

I should insert here that God's Word never returns void (Isa. 55:11). With every faith-sharing experience, regardless of how poorly I handled it, everyone was moved closer to Jesus. That was always amazing to me and taught me that God is in charge, and I'm merely His assistant.

WHAT'S GOD UP TO NOW?

Dave and Patti Holls were a couple we fell in love with the first time we met them at the Meadow Brook Concours in Detroit.

Dave had been one of the top designers at General Motors, was a great car collector, founded the Meadow Brook Concours with his buddy Don Sommers, and was chief judge of the honorary judges who picked "Best of Show" at the Pebble Beach Concours. He was bigger than life, a John Wayne-type character who was hugely respected throughout the car industry and the car hobby.

They were thirty years our senior with no apparent reason to become our close friends. But we became more than close, and the four of us had dinner together at car guy events all over the country. It's interesting how they were never comfortable with us talking about God or praying over our meals together. But our love for them was undaunted, and theirs for us.

I was the speaker at a church on a Sunday morning just ten minutes from their house. We had dinner the night before, and I was sure they would come, but they did not. Had I been speaking anywhere else other than a church, I had no doubt they would have come to hear me. During our dinner on the last night of the Amelia Island Concours over twenty years ago, Patti asked me to tell Dave he had to go to the doctor when he returned to Detroit. While he had not mentioned it, she was very concerned something was wrong in his throat. So I did, and he did, and he called me two weeks later to tell me he had stage 4 cancer with little time left to live.

That's why God put us together with this amazing couple who was far older than us. We loved them, prayed for them, and always made sure that everything we said and did was moving them closer to Jesus. They never had God in their lives, but through us they knew God was real. We threw out every kind of spiritual "chum" we could think of over a period of ten years, for this moment—and now he was ready.

On that very phone call, I led David Holls to the Lord. That only happened because of our years of allowing God to love Dave through us. During his last couple of weeks, he lost all interest in his cars and the car hobby. Patti called me on a Sunday morning asking me to pray for him to calm him down. She put him on the phone, and the Holy Spirit joined us as we had an amazing prayer time together. Dave died later that week, and Patti told me he was in complete peace from the time of our prayer to the moment he passed. My reminding him that he was on his way to heaven gave him complete peace for the last week of his life.

I had the privilege of speaking at his funeral to the royalty of the car industry, explaining Dave's rejection and then acceptance of God and that now he was in heaven. Then I prayed the sinner's prayer for all of them. Looking back, Dave and Patti only knew God by our love—and our love led Dave to Jesus.

Here's the most disturbing part of the story, which speaks loudly to the hold Satan has on us. In our continuing relationship with Patti, she still didn't want to talk about God and let us know she didn't want us to pray over our meals. After she watched the miracle of Dave accepting the Lord and asked me to speak at his funeral, she immediately returned to her normal godless life until she found out she had stage 4 cancer. We were in Detroit for the Meadowbrook Concours one day, had extra time, and called Patti just moments after she got the news to see if we could get together.

She asked if we could come immediately, and we did. Patti was in shock as she shared her story. We loved on her and prayed for her and led her to the Lord that day in her living room. God knew the hearts of these two precious people and supernaturally brought us into their lives so they could see Him face-to-face. He's so amazing! And we now get to spend eternity with Dave and Patti.

After sharing my faith on a daily basis for fifty years and processing every sermon and every scripture read through the lens of a faith sharer, you start to put all the pieces together. The interconnectedness of the Bible validates the truth that sharing our faith is the most integral part of our faith. We can't share what we don't have. But when we have wholehearted, unwavering faith, we can't stop from sharing it and enjoying it, because everything's possible for a person who believes (Mark 9:23, NLT).

On the one side, James 1 tells us that God's not obligated to answer our prayers when our faith is double-minded. On the other side, John 9:31 tells us: "We know that God doesn't listen to sinners, but he is ready to hear those who worship him and do his will" (NLT). It's fair to say that performing the Great Commission, loving our neighbors as ourselves, and living our lives for His purpose is "doing His will." I love knowing, for sure, that God is listening to my prayers!

We were at dinner one night with a wonderful couple, both of them car guys. The husband told me that if I wanted to get to our mutual friend Dave Robertson (a different Dave), I needed to act quickly. Turned out he had been diagnosed with stage 4 cancer, with little time left—and he wasn't telling anyone. An added note: my friend who was telling me this was not a Christian at the time.

I had a close relationship with Dave for more than thirty years in spite of the fact that he went out of his way to question everything I said about God. Every time we were together, the banter would begin. He wasn't mean; he just had a million questions that I always answered with humor and love. I seriously loved him, and he loved me. He was the classic high-IQ guy in search of truth who could not accept the simplicity of the Bible.

I immediately called him and invited him to lunch, and he couldn't say yes fast enough. Not wanting to betray the confidence, I let Dave tell me the bad news at his pace. Now I had his full attention, I had earned his trust over thirty years, he could not have been more receptive, and I led him to the Lord. Thirty years of lovingly answering his unending questions paid off. Even seed that falls on rocky ground can eventually take root (Matt. 13:5).

Dave called me the next day concerned that he didn't have a pastor or a place to hold his service. I told him I'd be honored to handle that for him. He asked if I would tell his unsaved friends that he had accepted the Lord and give them the opportunity to accept the Lord during his service. I did that, and four people raised their hands for salvation, including our mutual friend who told me over dinner that I needed to get to Dave. That's a twofer!

Before he died, I visited Dave lying in a hospice bed in his living room, and his wife said through her tears, "David, I don't want to lose you, but you know you never would have made it into heaven if it wasn't for this cancer." Dave was beyond talking, but he gave the sound of agreement when she said that, and we wept. It was a moment I'll never forget. And I get to spend eternity with my buddy Dave Robertson.

Sharing your faith is not a "Yikes!" It's a "Wow!"

SCRIPTURES FOR DEEPER REFLECTION

- **Faithfulness in the small things opens the door for God's trust and blessings:** Matthew 25:23 (NLT)

- **No more excuses; there's no training required to love on people:** John 13:35 (NIV)

- **Every faith-sharing experience, regardless how bad, leads people closer to Jesus:** Isaiah 55:11 (NKJV)

- **Sharing your faith explodes your faith with limitless possibilities:** John 9:31 (GW)

- **God listens to your prayers when you do His will— living for His purpose:** John 9:31 (NLT)

- **We never know how long it might take for the seed we sow to take root:** Matthew 13:5 (NIV)

CHAPTER 13

WHY THE MANDATE?

IN CASE YOU haven't noticed, this entire book is focused on God's mandate to move everyone, every day, closer to Jesus. Every chapter is intended to shout that message to you.

From thirty thousand feet, it's excruciatingly obvious that our world is sinking into depravity and Christians are sinking into paralysis for the very same reason: we've left our first love, and we're no longer doing the first work. Most Christians are focusing on doing good things to please God rather than focusing on God and His purpose. And it's the empty satisfaction from merely doing good things that has robbed the church of its joy.

We feel good about counseling young people on how to succeed in life, encouraging new mothers on how to be good mothers, supporting candidates who share our values, giving money to help feed the poor, and on and on. But you can do all of that and more without impressing God. Being a good person, doing good things, doesn't get you or anyone else into heaven. In fact, the world is full of good people doing good things that have nothing to do with God.

I've said it often, and it bears repeating: for those of us who are Christians, the only thing that will matter a hundred years from now is how many people will be in heaven because of our influence. Matthew 6:19–21 puts it in perspective: "Don't store up treasures here on earth, where moths eat them and rust destroys them, and where thieves break in and steal. Store your treasures in heaven, where moths and rust cannot destroy, and thieves do not break in and steal. Wherever your treasure is, there the desires of your heart will also be" (NLT). If you treasure the thought of seeing your unsaved friends and loved ones in heaven, that's where your heart will be!

When you treasure God, when you hold Him as your first love, the desire of your heart will be to do the first work: to please Him, to love Him, to live for His purpose, to tell everyone you can about Him. You're here on earth long enough to figure out who God is, commit your life to Him, and lead as many people as possible to Him before you see Him face-to-face.

On an earthly level, I can't say enough how much I love my business, which has put us right in the middle of the car hobby. Car guys make incredible friends, and Karen and I have them all over the world. Unfortunately, because of their goodness, many of them see themselves as being entitled to heaven and are the hardest to reach. This may be hard to understand. But we have car guy friends who, because of their goodness, are breaking our hearts.

Here's the crazy part. That same mindset has infiltrated the church. I'm not even sure what the term *Evangelical* means anymore. More than half of Evangelicals believe there are multiple ways to heaven and that good works are the essential ingredient.[1] That's what happens when most of our sermons are focused on how to be a better person, with less than 10 percent of our sermons even mentioning salvation.[2] How far we have fallen! Only 17 percent of regular church attenders say they've heard the term *Great Commission* and know what it means.[3] When's the last time your pastor mentioned the Great Commission or quoted Ephesians 4:11–12, "the role of the pastor...is to equip the saints for ministry"? Small wonder less than 10 percent of us are sharing our faith.[4]

Here's our reality check: almost 80 percent of our population is living outside the influence of the church.[5] They're scripturally referred to as nonbelievers, and here's what the Scriptures say about them: "The god of this age has blinded the minds of unbelievers, so that they cannot see the light of the gospel that displays the glory of Christ" (2 Cor. 4:4). This is the only explanation for all the lunatic decisions today. This is spiritual warfare, and it cannot be fought with politics and the minds of men and women.

So how can unbelievers become believers when they're not going to church? That's where the Great Commission comes in. That's our (your) job. The only hope for unbelievers is us! This is exactly what Romans 10:14–15 is saying: "But how can they call on him to save them unless they believe in him? And how can they believe in him if they have never heard about him? And how can they hear about him unless someone tells them? And how will anyone go and tell them without being sent?" (NLT). Our problem, pastors, is that you're not sending us!

One of the impediments to our being sent is that our pastors aren't sharing their faith. It's all but impossible to tell people how to do something that you don't know how to do yourself. Here's the enigma: most Christians believe faith sharing is their pastor's job, while most of our pastors never think about it.

How often I've been told by pastors that they don't have the opportunity to share their faith because they're surrounded by Christians. To which I reply, "Oh, you don't go to Starbucks, or the grocery store, or restaurants, or waiting rooms, or speak to operators on the phone?" Pastors, you need to model in your life what we should be doing in ours. Great church services are worthless if they're not provoking us to action. I know this is letting the chips fall! But church, we have to start *being* the church and stop sitting on the bench, watching and complaining about how the game is being played from the sidelines. Every one of us should be changing our worlds!

Let me be abundantly simplistic. Forgetting the second work of grace for a moment, there are two steps to being a Christian: join the team and play your position (wherever God has planted you) as well as it can be played. Most Christians join the team and sit on the bench, bored out of their minds and complaining about everything. Just saying!

**JOIN THE TEAM
AND PLAY YOUR
POSITION**
————

Some of us are loud, some of us are not. Some of us have huge responsibilities, and some of us don't. Some of us are highly educated, and some of us are uneducated. Some of us have been in church all our lives, and some of us have just started attending. The good news is that God loves us all the same, and He has a specific position He wants you to play. He needs your voice to reach those who will not listen to my voice but will listen to yours. You've got game! And you're right where God wants you!

I often say, "When you least expect a faith-sharing opportunity, expect it." I was in Detroit staying at the Downtown Marriott, a ten-minute walk from the convention center where Autorama was taking place. But it was seven degrees outside, and I chose to take a taxi. When I got in the taxi, I immediately told the driver I just needed a short ride but I'd give him a big tip, and he yelled, "I don't want a tip!" I said, "Excuse me, why don't you want a tip?" He said, "I'm a bad person—I don't deserve a tip."

The pressure of sharing my faith ended years earlier when I discovered Luke 12:12: "For the Holy Spirit will teach you at that time what needs to be said" (NLT). In this case, the Holy Spirit prompted me to say, "Do you know God loves you?" and he yelled, "No!" I said again, "Oh yes, God loves you!" and he yelled again, "No!" Then I said, "Sir, I'm a Christian and a student of the Bible, and I can tell you for sure, God loves you!"

This time he said nothing, and I continued. "In fact, God loves you as much as He's ever loved anyone." Still dead silence. He had no idea what to say. The thought that God loved him was obviously overwhelming for him. I said, "God loves you as much as He loves His own Son, Jesus Christ." Crickets. Nothing. Nada. The weight of what I had just told him struck him dumb. You know, most people can't believe God loves them after all they've done in their lives. They think God's mad at them!

By then we were at the convention center. I got out and walked to his passenger window. You could hear the salt on the glass as he put down the window, and I could see his blank face. I said to him, "God put me in your taxi because He wants you to know that He loves you. And He wants you to spend eternity with Him." The expression on his face was one of absolute shock. I handed him a big tip and said, "Have a great day—God bless you!" And I walked off with a bounce in my step as I looked up and saw Jesus smiling down at me. "The joy of the LORD is [my] strength" (Neh. 8:10).

GIVING GOD JOY

Did you know you can give God joy? You can grieve Him, or you can give Him joy. And it's His joy, not mine, that gives me strength. There's nothing like knowing you just did exactly what He wanted you to do. And I experience that on a regular basis. People often ask me why I'm so happy all the time. The reason is that I'm always just coming off of one of these experiences, and I know God already has another one headed my way. Isn't it interesting that the one thing we don't want to do, that we dread having to do, is the one thing that turns every day into an adventure?

This poor man may have been about to commit suicide. Who knows? If I had not been thinking spiritually, I may have wanted to escape that car before he killed himself and me with him. But I knew it was a divine appointment, and I was ready to give a clear presentation of the hope that's within me (1 Pet. 3:15). Who knows, maybe he's preaching the gospel somewhere today. This I do know—I used my five minutes with him to move him closer to Jesus.

Think about the 120 people who gathered in that Upper Room, who were anointed with the Holy Spirit and changed the world forever. They didn't have churches or Bibles or evangelism training programs. What they had was first-generation zeal for God that they couldn't share fast enough. If you like to compare your love and obedience to God with others, this is the target group you want to imitate. In fact, the apostle Paul actually instructs us to imitate him just as he in turn imitates Christ (1 Cor. 4:16).

The disconnect most Christians have between their faith and their everyday lives today is staggering. Most are far more energized over what's happening in DC, or at their job, or in their relationships than in what's happening in their own relationship with God or whether those around them are headed to heaven. I'm amazed at how often Christians tell me they don't know when I ask if their friend is a Christian. What they're saying is, "I don't care."

Each of us has our own thoughts on when the rapture is going to happen. I suspect it's going to happen "soon and very soon." Think of all the unsaved friends and loved ones you have in your life who will be left behind if it does happen soon. If you knew the rapture was going to happen tomorrow, what would you be saying to your unsaved friends today? Your goal should be to live every day as if the rapture is going to happen tomorrow. Their eternity may depend on you doing that. It probably won't. But what if it does?

I want to end this chapter with one of the most compelling reasons there is for sharing your faith. It speaks to your personal preparation for what's ahead of you. It's more than possible that Christians in America will be persecuted for their faith before the rapture. If you're already living in fear, along with more than 80 percent of all Christians, you need to fix that!

Most of God's promises and blessings are tied to trusting Him with wholehearted faith that comes by sharing your faith. The Book of Revelation is quite clear on what lies ahead of us, and the signs of the times have already begun. Luke 21:28 tells us: "And when these things *begin* to come to pass, then look up, and lift up your heads; for your redemption draweth nigh" (KJV, emphasis added). It's been said the darker it gets, the closer we are to seeing Jesus.

In preparation for when Satan is on full attack mode against the church, Revelation 12:11 tells us exactly how we are to survive these last days. This is one of the most powerful and important scriptures in the entire Bible: "They triumphed over [Satan] by the blood of the Lamb and by the *word of their testimony*; they did not love their lives so much as to shrink from death" (Rev. 12:11, emphasis added).

This is how we are to live our lives for the rest of our lives!

SCRIPTURES FOR DEEPER REFLECTION

- **The only thing you can treasure now and in heaven is those you lead to Jesus:** Matthew 6:19–21 (NLT)

- Only 10 percent of our pulpits are "equipping the saints" (us) for ministry: Ephesians 4:11–12 (ESV)

- Insane decisions are made by unbelievers blinded by Satan: 2 Corinthians 4:4 (NIV)

- Here's the problem—pastors have stopped sending us to reach the lost: Romans 10:14–15 (NLT)

- The pressure is off when the Holy Spirit is giving you the words to say: Luke 12:12 (NLT)

- Knowing that sharing your faith gives God joy makes life bigger than life: Nehemiah 8:10 (NKJV)

- Always being ready to share God's love keeps you gentle and respectful: 1 Peter 3:15 (NIV)

- Comparing yourself to Paul and the apostles will keep you humble: 1 Corinthians 4:16 (NIV)

- End-time prophecies are already being fulfilled: Luke 21:28 (KJV)

- Your faith and testimony will get you through whatever lies ahead: Revelation 12:11 (NIV)

CHAPTER 14

EXERCISE DISCERNMENT

DICTIONARIES DEFINE *DISCERNMENT* as the ability to recognize small details, accurately tell the difference between similar things, and make intelligent judgments. It's the polar opposite of being gullible. That's why discernment is part of the long list of gifts God gives to the church. Hebrews 5:14 explains that discernment comes with spiritual maturity: "solid food belongs to those who are of full age, that is, those who by reason of use have their senses exercised to discern both good and evil" (NKJV).

On a practical basis, our greatest resource for discernment is the Word of God. Hebrews 4:12 tells us: "For the word of God is alive and active. Sharper than any double-edged sword, it penetrates even to dividing soul and spirit, joints and marrow; it judges the thoughts and attitudes of the heart."

Here's the problem. With only 51 percent of our pastors still holding a biblical worldview,[1] you have no way of knowing if a minister (or friend) is providing you with scriptural truth or their personal bias if you don't know the Word of God for yourself. How can you discern truth from error? You can't! Sadly, despite the overabundance of information available these days, most Christians are biblically illiterate and unable to tell truth from fiction, biblical truth from Satan's lies.

If Christians simply knew the Scriptures, they would discern our times. Bible prophecy explains everything that's happening to America and the world today. "The Spirit clearly says that in later times some will abandon the faith and follow deceiving spirits and things taught by demons" (1 Tim. 4:1). We're now seeing this with our own eyes as Christians and pastors and even denominations are losing their discernment and turning their backs on biblical truth. I keep asking myself, How is that possible?

Contrary to popular thinking, Satan is the "god" of this world. Second Corinthians 4:4 clearly states, "Satan, who is the god of this world, has blinded the minds of those who don't believe" (NLT). God has allowed Satan to be the god of this world for as long as it serves His plan. And Christians, for a host of reasons, are losing their discernment and flat-out allowing Satan to distract them from God's plan for their life and the world.

Almost every decision you make requires discernment between what is good and what is best. When something becomes more important to you than God, regardless of how wonderful and righteous it might be, it's a victory for Satan, and he'll take full advantage. He'll use whatever it takes to separate you from God, capture your heart, and—if you let him—destroy your soul. And he's unrelenting! He never stops.

SEEK THE GIFT OF DISCERNMENT

The primary thing Satan wants to do is undermine the authority of God's Word in your mind and keep you from studying and knowing it. If he can accomplish that, he can keep you undiscerning and unleash all sorts of half-truths and false teachings into your life.

LACK OF DISCERNMENT

For lack of discernment, well-meaning Christians, pastors, and even denominations are adopting the false doctrines of Christians, pastors, and academics who have departed from the truth. It's called collective rationalization, or "GroupThink," when groups of people rationalize together to the wrong conclusion. We now find ourselves surrounded with vehement support for ungodly issues by those who once stood with us.

We tend to become like those with whom we spend our time. When biblically illiterate Christians spend time with other biblically illiterate Christians, their faith is easily polluted with fears, worries, false doctrines, activities, and indulgences that are in contradiction with the Word of God. It's the blind leading the blind when new or infant Christians follow the advice of those who themselves are unable to discern good from evil.

This is not a small issue. Only 21 percent of Evangelicals still hold a biblical worldview.[2] Without understanding from your own Bible study what God's Word actually says, it's all but impossible to know when someone is expressing God's truth or Satan's lies. And God is holding you accountable for knowing the difference. Good intentions are worthless unless they're biblically based. There has never been a more important time for you to discern the truth of God's Word and the depth, or lack thereof, to which it is being lived out in the lives of those around you.

If we're truly in the last days, all of us need to be at the top of our game for ourselves and for each other going forward. Colossians 3:16 tells us: "Let the word of Christ dwell in you richly, teaching and admonishing one another in all wisdom, singing psalms and hymns and spiritual songs, with thankfulness in your hearts to God" (ESV).

Most Americans still self-identify as being Christians, with most of them having no idea what that means. But it sounds good and gains them respect. They'll speak of the "Big Guy in the sky" or the "higher power," without knowing how quickly that reveals their ignorance of God.

But then there are the wolves in sheep's clothing that have "Christian speak" mastered. They look and sound like solid, Bible-believing, Christ-honoring Christians, with enough Scripture to gain credibility. They love going to church and gaining recognition in the church. But if you listen carefully and exercise your discernment, the Holy Spirit will warn you to be wary.

When threatened by the Romans in the first centuries after Christ, Christians used the sign of the fish to mark meeting places and tombs, or to distinguish friends from foes. If two men met on a road, discerning each other to be Christians, one would draw an arc in the dirt, and the other would complete the arc to make the sign of a fish. The reference, of course, was to Jesus telling us we are to be fishers of men. Then they knew it was safe to talk.

This is a real-life issue for over 300 million Christians today who are living under persecution, many of them facing death if they're discovered. And while this level of persecution is still far from us, knowing who is with us and who you can trust for sound doctrine and godly advice is going to become increasingly important in the days ahead.

Your gift of discernment needs to be exercised!

SCRIPTURES FOR DEEPER REFLECTION

- **Discernment comes with spiritual maturity:** Hebrews 5:14 (NKJV)

- **It has never been more important to know the Word of God personally:** Hebrews 4:12 (NIV)

- **Most Christians are biblically illiterate and unable to tell truth from fiction:** 1 Timothy 4:1 (NIV)

- **Over 80 percent of our population are unbelievers, blinded by Satan and unable to see truth:** 2 Corinthians 4:4 (NLT)

- **The Word of God is your ultimate defense against the lies of Satan:** Colossians 3:16 (ESV)

CHAPTER 15

IT'S A TEAM SPORT!

WITH GREAT SENSITIVITY to the heaven-or-hell consequences of sharing your faith, it's helpful for you to know that when you do share your faith, you're in a team sport. You're never alone.

When I first started sharing my faith, I thought I always had to close the sale, so to speak, in one setting. And because that rarely happens, I was a defeated faith sharer from the very beginning. Seriously, I thought I was a failure, and I never wanted to do that again. And no one told me any differently.

"Time schedule faith sharing" ignores everything the Scriptures have to say on the subject. There's no time schedule for leading people to Jesus for a variety of reasons. Some of those are described by Jesus in His parable of the sower in Matthew 13:1–8 (MEV):

> Listen! A sower went out to sow. While he sowed, some seeds fell beside the path, and the birds came and devoured them. But other seeds fell on rocky ground where they did not have much soil, and immediately they sprang up because they did not have deep soil. But when the sun rose, they were scorched. And because they did not take root, they withered away. Some seeds fell among thorns, and the thorns grew up and choked them. But other seeds fell into good ground and produced grain: a hundred, sixty, or thirty times as much.

You see, it's not about you. No matter what you say, it's being received by people who are all over the place in their spiritual journey. I was checking in curbside at the Orange County airport when the skycap excitedly told me he was starting his own business. And then he asked, "Mr. Meguiar, what's the best piece of advice you can give me to be successful?" I immediately said, "That's easy." I asked if he had a Bible at home, and he answered yes. I said, "Great. Go to Proverbs 3:5; it's my life verse, and I've built my company on it. It says if you trust God with your whole heart, He'll direct your steps." The guy said, "Wow, I'll read it as soon as I get home!" For years I had built my relationship with this skycap through good tips and saying "God bless you" and loving on him. And that ultimately gave me the credibility to give him advice that might change his life.

The best part was that an Orange County sheriff was standing about fifteen feet away leaning against a post. And while I was talking, I watched her body posture lean in my direction so she could hear my advice. Many times I'm speaking to others who are listening as much as I'm speaking to the person I'm addressing. I call that a "twofer."

Some are just a step away, and some are a mile away from making their decision. To suggest that we can bring everyone to a saving knowledge of Jesus Christ in one setting should never have been taught in the church. But it was—with spillover into today. I'm amazed at how many Christians today still believe sharing their faith should always end with the person on their knees praying the sinner's prayer. That alone stops people from sharing their faith!

First of all, we can't save anyone. Our job is to simply lead those around us into God's presence, with love, at every opportunity. And the estimates range from eight to twenty spiritual encounters, on average, being required before most people are ready to accept the Lord.

Some of the people we share our faith with are "fertile ground," and some are not. Only God knows where each person is on their spiritual journey. I have people I've been sharing my faith with for twenty years without results, while others have been ready to make the decision before I opened my mouth. So it's pointless to have a one-size-fits-all script to recite to every unbeliever, thinking it will always lead them to the Lord in one step. It doesn't work that way. And understanding it doesn't work that way takes a load of pressure off you.

In fact, any pressure you feel related to sharing your faith is entirely self-imposed. God does all the work. He makes the divine appointments, and He gives you the words to say when you need them. When you're nervous, you'll talk too much and say all the wrong things. And it comes across as a sales pitch! But when you're genuinely loving on people, allowing God to give you the right words, everything you say has an anointing on it that changes lives. That's when your intimacy with God ignites your life. There's no other human experience that rivals it.

THE PRESSURE IS OFF

The concept of team sport faith sharing is presented and affirmed even more clearly in 1 Corinthians 3:6–9:

> I planted the seed, Apollos watered it, but God has been making it grow. So neither the one who plants nor the one who waters is anything, but only God, who makes things grow. The one who plants and the one who waters have one purpose, and they will each be rewarded according to their own labor. For we are co-workers in God's service; you are God's field, God's building.

Notice that those leading people to Jesus are *rewarded according to their own labor.* When we're leading people to Jesus, we're storing up for ourselves treasures in heaven. Unfortunately, it won't matter how many bottles of car wax I sold when I get to heaven. The only thing that will matter is how many people will be in heaven because of my influence. Can you imagine the joy you'll have seeing people in heaven because of your influence?

I walked into a restaurant yesterday with a very nervous young man starting his first day on the job at that restaurant. He was anxiously reviewing his written instructions before he walked through the front door with me, apologizing and explaining his distraction. I watched his body posture as he nervously reported for duty to the manager—and God gave me a nudge.

I walked across the restaurant and politely interrupted their conversation. I asked for his name, and he said, "Thomas." Then I said, "Thomas, our entire group was impressed with you when we walked in the front door with you, and we decided we wanted to get your name so we could pray for you on your first day of work." Neither Thomas nor the manager knew how to say thank you enough. Then we told our waiter about Thomas and asked if there was anything we could pray for him about.

I didn't lead Thomas to the Lord. I have no idea where he is on his faith journey. But with God nudging me, I seized the moment, and there's no question I moved Thomas, the manager, and our waiter closer to Jesus—and it took maybe five minutes. More importantly, I knew I was planting seeds that will be cultivated and watered by other "team members" (Christians) I will never know.

You may only say one God-inspired comment to someone that confirms what they just heard from another Christian during a two-hour conversation. When you're in the game, these kinds of experiences become routine and affirming to you that He's directing your steps. You're in the game, it's a team sport, and we're playing to win!

Some might say that it's sacrilege to connect *sport* with leading people to Jesus. And some people believe Jesus never smiled. But Jesus said: "I tell you, there is rejoicing in the presence of the angels of God over one sinner who repents" (Luke 15:10). And I have a hard time believing the angels only know the end of the story. I suspect they're following the progress and cheering on every unbeliever who's coming to God.

I'm going off the chart here without any scriptural support at all, but I suspect there are cheering sections on both sides of every salvation experience. And the cheers coming from the angels, in my mind, seriously compel me to do whatever it takes to lead an unbeliever to the Lord. And then I for sure celebrate with them afterward. All of this takes sharing my faith into being the most exciting and most rewarding part of my life.

I'm a bit of a sports nut and marvel at how the best players are always on their toes, always ready to drive to the basket at the slightest opening or make the heroic throw to first base for the double-play. They're playing the game, but they're playing to win.

That's how God wants us to live our lives spiritually. We're playing the game of life, but we're playing to win souls.

A NEW CONCEPT

I know it's an entirely new concept and the opposite of what you've been taught, but faith sharing is not hard, and it's not about telling people what they don't want to know, and it's not about being persecuted. Religious persecution is out of control around the world and is now coming to America. But I've been sharing my faith in America for almost fifty years, and I've never had a bad experience. People don't get mad at you when you tell them God loves them! It's actually fun to watch their reactions. Just allow God to love people through you. And when they want more, they'll ask. You can't force people into being Christians.

I'm continually looking for ways to inject God into every conversation, without raising eyebrows, without offending anyone. I do it with humor, and I do it playing off whatever is being said at the moment. It also keeps me focused and interested in what everyone else is saying *and* what they're not saying. What's behind their mask so I can connect with them on a heart-to-heart basis, to move them closer to Jesus? This is what loving our neighbors as ourselves looks like. Your job is to play your position the best you can possibly play it, seizing every opportunity to move everyone, every day, closer to Jesus.

I met Judy at a ladies' prayer retreat at our house one weekend. She has more of Jesus than I do, so I quickly gravitated to her and found myself growing in the Lord just talking with her. It's a good idea to spend as much time as possible with people who love the Lord as much or more than you. They pull you up; most people don't. Two weeks later her son, Brandon, whom I did not know, called me on a Saturday morning from Dallas. He introduced himself and told me the miracle story of his meeting for the first time and leading a Jewish-Canadian man to the Lord that morning. It was an excellent example of an unbeliever who was primed by others and ready for ignition. And now this man was heading for the Dallas/Fort Worth airport to fly to Phoenix.

Brandon called his mom (Judy) and asked her if she knew a Christian in Scottsdale (a suburb of Phoenix), and she gave him my name. It's a team sport! Two hours after he landed in Phoenix, this Jewish-Canadian new believer and I were having a two-hour lunch in Scottsdale, like we were old friends. He needed to have direction on his next steps. I explained how his spiritual life would be ignited into full bloom when he shared his salvation story with his unsaved friends. And he took it to heart. I've lost track of how many of his Canadian friends he's led to the Lord.

Let's follow the track. I meet Judy in Scottsdale. Her son in Dallas leads a stranger from Canada to the Lord. He calls me, a stranger, and asks me to pinch hit. I meet with this Jewish-Canadian new believer four hours later in Scottsdale. I explain to him how sharing his faith will keep him ignited, and now he's leading people to the Lord in Canada. It's a team sport!

Most of the time we'll not know, until we get to heaven, how many people ministered to the same people as us. I occasionally reconnect with people who were with me when I shared with one of their friends, and they tell me how that person finally accepted the Lord years later. I usually don't remember. When you're doing it every day, it's hard to remember everyone. But God remembers everyone who played a part in every person's salvation.

I was flying to Springfield, Missouri, to see George Wood, the former general superintendent of the Assemblies of God, who was dying from stage 4 cancer. I was flying between Christmas and New Year's to have my last conversation with George. We had done so much together, traveled together, walked the footsteps of Paul together, shared platforms together, challenged each other spiritually together, and laughed together for decades. We were buddies.

I knew it was my last chance to see him. It was a busy time, but I had to do it. I normally travel with Karen, but not this time. She was in the middle of family and Christmas. I was sitting in my window seat when a colorful, happy guy sat down beside me.

Turned out he owned a charter boat company in Florida. I could have guessed that by his deeply tanned skin, golden hair, and resort attire.

We began talking immediately. He was great fun, and our conversation was effortless. Of course, I watched for the first opportunity to inject God into our conversation. He was entirely open and had studied most religions, being turned off by Christian churches that he described as "businesses only after his money." I told him that was a turnoff for me too, as well as for God. God just wants to love us into eternity.

In the middle of the flight, he communicated with his wife, who was sitting one row behind us, across the aisle, by the window. Then he turned to me and asked if I knew who Tim Tebow was. Of course, I said yes. Then he quoted his wife as saying Tim Tebow was sitting next to her. I immediately looked back, and Tim's eyes were transfixed on me. As I looked at him, I raised one finger to say, "One way," and he did the same. I finished the flight praying for my new boat charter friend as we were landing. Then I gave him one of our "Seeking God" cards that can lead unbelievers from no knowledge to salvation.

When I got off the plane, I waited for Tim. When he walked off, he came right to me. I had to ask him if he was really Tim Tebow because he was wearing a mask. He said yes, and I told him how much I respected him and followed him and prayed for him. And then I mentioned how I was witnessing to my seatmate. He said, "I know, I was listening to you. And when you looked at me raising your finger, it hit me you have the husband, I have the wife. So I witnessed to his wife for the entire last half of our flight."

That was a divine appointment! God loved that couple so much that He split them up on the airplane and had both of them sit next to Christians who were locked and loaded, ready to lead them to Jesus. You have no idea how much fun you're going to have when you get off the bench and into the game.

It's a team sport!

SCRIPTURES FOR DEEPER REFLECTION

- **Salvation rarely occurs with one conversation:** Matthew 13:1–9 (MEV)

- **Here's a great Scripture verse for those seeking wisdom:** Proverbs 3:5 (ISV)

- **Every faith-sharing experience involves a team—with eternal rewards:** 1 Corinthians 3:6–9 (NIV)

- **Every person's salvation brings celebration:** Luke 15:10 (NIV)

CHAPTER 16

DOES GOD DIRECT YOUR STEPS?

THE CLOSER YOU get to God and live your life for His purpose, the more you understand that the entirety of Scripture is interrelated and interdependent. For example, God working everything in your life for good depends on your living for His purpose to bring people to Him, which leads to the redemption of mankind. It's amazing how "Christians" can be Christian all their lives and be totally oblivious to the entire reason for their being alive and breathing—living for themselves and the things of this world.

Knowing that God is making everything in your life work for good is the foundation for living your life by faith, not by sight (2 Cor. 5:7). We're called "people of faith," and we know that "without faith it is impossible to please God" (Heb. 11:6). When we're worrying, we're not "faithing," and God will let us flap in the wind until we grow weary and come back to Him. Failing to trust Him to direct your steps removes His obligation to direct your steps.

In car guy terms, God wants to be the steering wheel of your life. But He can't lead you if you're not moving. Your faith is the key that starts your engine and the foot that presses the accelerator. Wholehearted faith puts the pedal to the metal and takes you to places exceedingly, abundantly beyond anything you could ask for or imagine (Eph. 3:20). Every day is an adventure when you're flat-out following God's lead. There's nothing in your human planning that can match what God has planned for you. I can't believe where He's taken us and how much fun we've had on the journey.

As a reminder, when Karen and I got married, I was part of a tiny family business selling a car wax no one had ever heard of by buffing cars in car dealerships and body shops. There's no way we could have imagined we'd become the top-selling car wax in the retail market with the opportunities we've been given to learn, experience, and share God's love with the lost.

Romans 8:11 tells us how this is possible: "The Spirit of God, who raised Jesus from the dead, lives in you" (NLT). You have no idea of the plans God has for you, or the power He wants to unleash through you, until you become one with Him, living for His purpose—to seek and save the lost. Paul explains it well in 2 Corinthians 4:13: "Since we have that same spirit of faith, we also believe and therefore speak." If we don't know it, we can't speak it. But if we do—look out!

American Christians have been over-educated with scriptures without needing to understand and rely on their power. We haven't needed to overcome the adversities that most Christians have faced all their lives. Millions of Christians around the world meet in home groups and churches knowing it could cost them their lives.

Because of their persecution, they trust the same scriptures with their lives that we know and doubt. Otherwise, we wouldn't be worrying! When you're with them, you're convicted by their unwavering faith and joy that's all but impossible to achieve without persecution. But it is possible.

For American Christians, the scriptures have been nice to know and quote but almost irrelevant to our daily lives. That's why, with the first signs of persecution, we hid in our homes, stopped going to church, and started worrying about everything. More than 80 percent of Americans, including Christians, are living in fear today.[1] That's Satan sterilizing Christians so they can't reproduce. When you're living in fear, you've lost your faith, and you can't share what you don't have. Our world is falling deeper into darkness by the day because of our inability to reproduce ourselves.

Without having gone through persecution, American Christians have been an easy target, staying mute as godless forces have turned America into a godless country. For the first time, American Christians have been challenged to decide between fearing man or fearing God. And except for a few voices in the wilderness, we've completely failed that challenge. Even now, deep into spiritual warfare, most Christians are sitting on the bench, complaining about everything and doing nothing.

On a personal basis, God has plans for you and wants to direct your steps. But it's your choice whether you want to follow Him or follow those who oppose Him. I'm reminded of the message in Matthew 6:24 that warns us: "No man can serve two masters: for either he will hate the one, and love the other; or else he will hold to the one, and despise the other. Ye cannot serve God and mammon" (KJV). As if He was thinking about America at this moment in time, Jesus told us in Matthew 12:25 that "every kingdom divided against itself is brought to desolation, and every city or house divided against itself shall not stand" (KJV).

IT'S YOUR CHOICE

Satan is showing up in public school curriculums, after-school "Satan clubs" are proliferating, and Satanists are fasting and praying for our demise. With Satan being the god of this world, we're seeing unprecedented divisions among us in every area of our lives, including our denominations, seminaries, churches, and worst of all, our families. Satan's on top of his game!

When things were going well, you could skate by rather easily enjoying a casual relationship with God. Nothing was driving you to your knees and into His Word to build your faith. But those days are gone forever. Most Christians now find themselves unprepared, sterilized with fear, with wavering faith at best, and no longer able to hear God's voice. God is decidedly not directing their steps. That's not where you want to be with Satan in full attack and God about to unleash the Antichrist on the world.

This is a wake-up call for those who don't love God more than everything else in their lives and are not living their lives for Him. If this describes you, you're robbing yourself of God's promise to hear and answer your prayers (Jas. 1:7), to direct your steps (Prov. 3:6), and to make everything in your life work for good (Rom. 8:28). Other than putting your head in the sand, ignoring all the facts, or truly believing that you know better than God what's best for you, why would you go another moment without telling God you're all-in on His plan for your life?

Psalm 37:23 tells us, "The steps of a good man are ordered by the LORD, and He delights in his way" (NKJV). Can you imagine anything greater than having the God who created the universe taking special interest in you, down to directing your steps into His perfect plan for your life? What could prevent you from wanting to do everything possible to make that happen? And why would you not follow His lead, building up treasures in heaven?

When my dad hit his eighties, I knew his time for formulating our products was coming to an end. Not being chemists themselves, both my dad and his dad relied on God's inspiration when they created their formulas. Now I had to find our next-generation chemist who could do the same thing. This was the biggest "new hire" challenge of my life.

I went to the top head-hunter agency in the country, who gave me over one hundred candidates that I eventually reduced to twenty-four, and then twelve, and then two. My challenge was that the best candidate, by far, was not a Christian, and I knew we couldn't rely on man's knowledge to keep making the best products on the market.

Throughout the process, I was committed to letting God direct my steps. I kept waiting for a "check," and it never came. It finally came down to the day when I was going to hire Gary, and I told God, "If he's not the one You want me to hire, cause it not to happen." I was going against all of my spiritual instincts to hire a non-Christian to replace my dad as our head chemist. But I was also giving God every opportunity to stop me, and He did not. So I hired Gary, and within six months he accepted Jesus Christ as his Lord and Savior, and we were back to trusting God for our formulations.

Going back to 1973, I closed my office door that day thinking I should leave my beloved business and asked God to confirm my thoughts that I should become a pastor. My reasoning was, How could God not be in favor of my leaving my business and becoming a pastor? It seemed so right and God-honoring in my mind.

But He directed Dave McNutt into my office just twenty minutes later to tell me, "Your business is your pulpit." Had He not directed Dave's steps to my office and my steps to stay with my business, I would have leaned unto my own understanding and been a terrible pastor. But I'm a businessman. It's true! *The steps of the righteous are ordered by the Lord.* And by the way, our righteousness is as filthy rags, but He clothes us in His righteousness when we accept Jesus Christ as our Savior and Lord.

From college, my life scripture has been Proverbs 3:5–6: "Trust in the LORD with all your heart, and lean not on your own understanding. In all your ways acknowledge Him, and He shall direct your paths." And guess what? It works!

EVEN WHEN YOUR CAR BREAKS DOWN

And it works both ways. God also directs the steps of those seeking Him. Karen and I took our 1901 Duryea to a local car show. It was only two miles away, so we decided to drive it. But on the way home, it gave up on us and quit. We both laughed and said, "God must be up to something!" Sure enough, a young man stopped, offered his help, and pulled us with his car to our garage.

In our house he noticed our lit cross hanging on the wall over a large open Bible from the 1800s. He excitedly asked if we were Christians and knew of a church he could attend. He was new to the area, was missing church, and had no idea where to go. The next morning, he attended his first Protestant church with us and fell in love. Amazingly, Tommy Barnett preached that morning on "So That," meaning whenever things go wrong, they go wrong "so that" God can work a miracle. This young man knew our 1901 Duryea broke down *so that* he could find his church. We both knew God had directed our steps. *And* Tommy Barnett's message on "So That" confirmed it.

With so many decisions to make on a given day, it's easy to make some of them without waiting for God's direction. I daresay it's normal to do that, but that doesn't make it right. And it's on those occasions that I have reasoned to the wrong conclusions and missed God's best for my life, even in the smallest of things.

Fortunately, God knows when our hearts are committed to Him. Proverbs 19:21 is incredibly comforting to me: "Many are the plans in a person's heart, but it is the LORD's purpose that prevails."

Allow the Lord's purpose to prevail in your life by allowing God to direct your steps!

SCRIPTURES FOR DEEPER REFLECTION

- **Beware of living/making decisions based only on what you see:** 2 Corinthians 5:7 (NIV)

- **God rewards you when you trust Him/seek Him and lead people to Him:** Hebrews 11:6 (NIV)

- **Always give God the glory for "salvationing" people through you:** Ephesians 3:20 (NLT)

- **The same power that raised Jesus from the dead is powering you!** Romans 8:11 (NLT)

- **If your faith is real, you'll speak it:** 2 Corinthians 4:13 (ESV)

- **Who's your God?** Matthew 6:24 (KJV)

- **This describes what's happening in America:** Matthew 12:25 (KJV)

- **Don't rob yourself of God's promise to hear and answer your prayers:** James 1:7 (NLT)

- **God makes all things good when you seek and save the lost:** Romans 8:28 (NIV)

- **Fear is defeated when you know that God is directing your steps:** Psalm 37:23 (KJV)

- God directs your steps when you glorify Him—in the good times and the bad: Proverbs 3:5–6 (NKJV)

- You have no idea the plans God has for you: Proverbs 19:21 (NIV)

CHAPTER 17

FOLLOW THE NUDGE; LIVE IN THE FOG

IN THE EARLY days of our Ignite America ministry, we had a display booth at the Assemblies of God biennial General Council. During the first day, Tom Trask, general superintendent of the Assemblies, stopped by to ask lots of questions. Years earlier he had presented me with the General Council's Layman of the Year Award. We were friends.

When Brother Trask gets excited, his face turns red and the blood vessels on his neck expand. He's a powerful man of God. After the service that night, he excused himself from a group and made a beeline for me. I was sure I was in trouble. Then he held my face and said, "God gave me this message for you! You're living in the FOG." I was certain he was telling me I didn't have a clue what I was doing and, as a layman, I shouldn't be there. My heart was pounding. Then he said, "My son, you're living in the favor of God."

For weeks after, and even until today, that term has intrigued me. So often I see God working miracles in people's lives and ministries, and I tell them, "You're living in the FOG." It's obvious that God is working miracles on their behalf. Most people who know me know I love that term. But how do we get there? It has nothing to do with our goodness or talents or accomplishments. I know it when I see it, but how do people and ministries get to where they're living in the favor of God?

On our IgniteAmerica.com website, I interview people of all types and descriptions who are ardent faith sharers. I want people to understand that most faith sharers don't look or sound like me. God uses each of us in our own unique way. The Great Commission doesn't say "Go ye" to any certain type of person. God has called all of us to share our faith.

One particular interview opened my eyes to a profound truth. Because of her passion, we asked an elderly Black lady to speak directly to the camera rather than be interviewed. Then I wept as I listened to her describe my relationship to God. She was expressing deep thoughts that I had never shared with anyone. How could it be that this precious lady, with decidedly different life experiences, was in such one accord with me? And it hit me. The closer we get to God, the closer we are to each other and to becoming the "body of Christ"!

As it happens, she lives in Fresno, California, and I live in Arizona, but we're family and couldn't be closer. Those who not only know the Word but live the Word are God's family of believers, closer than brothers. The Bible calls us the body of Christ, and what a beautiful description that is. All of us are different parts of the body of Christ. All of us are assigned to different positions on the playing field, privileged to represent Christ during these last and final days of mankind.

I'm still amazed at how often I'm described as a "religious person." Anyone using that language, regardless of how well intended, is revealing their complete misunderstanding of who God is and how He works. Religion is man's attempt to earn God's favor—which is impossible! We can't earn His favor. "For it is by grace you have been saved, through faith—and this is not from yourselves, it is the gift of God" (Eph. 2:8). Our relationship with God has nothing to do with what we do and everything to do with what Jesus Christ did for us on the cross.

This is why being a good person and doing good things doesn't get you or anyone else into heaven. While it makes you feel good and makes people like you, it has nothing to do with redemption. When you simply do good things, all the glory goes to you. There are millions of good people doing good things who have no relationship with God. Unfortunately, many of them believe they're going to heaven because they're such good people. That's a widespread deception from the pit of hell.

Here's a simple question: If we could earn our way into heaven, why did Jesus Christ go through the horrific agony of the cross, giving His life as a sacrifice for our sins? Jesus made it very clear in John 14:6: "I am the way and the truth and the life. No one comes to the Father except through me." While it's widely believed both inside and outside the church, believing you can earn your way into heaven is the outright rejection of Jesus Christ's sacrificing His life for you.

Isaiah 64:6 says that "all our righteous acts are like filthy rags." Romans 3:10 tells us, "There is none righteous, no, not even one" (NKJV). You may feel good when comparing yourself to those around you, even Christians. But God's judgment is based on His pureness and holiness and complete intolerance of sin. That's why the only way to get into heaven is by receiving forgiveness of our sins and being clothed in His righteousness, justified through the death and resurrection of our Savior and Lord, Jesus Christ.

The favor of God begins with making Jesus Christ the Lord of your life. Not just with words, but by everything you do and say for the rest of your life. If He's not your Lord, you won't serve Him, things will not go well for you, and you may eventually depart from Him. You need to be all-in! As they say, you can't be a little bit pregnant. This is what takes you into a personal relationship with God that is unquestionably supernatural.

God made us different from the animals with our body, soul, and spirit, which is God's point of contact with us. In our triune God, we have God the Father, God the Son, and God the Holy Spirit, who communes with us through our spirit, convicts us, empowers us, and leads us to Jesus. It's the spirit part of our being that deserves our greatest attention. God told us in Hebrews 13:5 that "I will never leave you nor forsake you" (NKJV). When things go south, God never says, "Oops." In fact, in Matthew 28:20, Jesus said, "I am with you always, even to the end of the age" (NLT). If you want to have a successful life full of faith and joy, you want your spirit to be led by the power of the Holy Spirit.

As bizarre as it sounds, God wants to have a personal relationship with you, with the only limitation being you. You can only begin to understand the vastness of God when you realize that He's offered this same personal relationship to everyone on planet Earth. The fact that He knows your every thought, even the number of hairs on your head, and still loves you as much as He loves His own Son, Jesus Christ, is beyond man's ability to comprehend.

David takes it even further in Psalm 139:17–18 when he says: "How precious are your thoughts about me, O God. They cannot be numbered! I can't even count them; they outnumber the grains of sand! And when I wake up, you are still with me!" (NLT). I can't get away from the thought that His thoughts are always on me. Always! This completely redefines our understanding of a personal relationship.

But it gets far better. God Almighty, who speaks worlds into existence, wants to be your best friend! He tells you how you can make that happen in John 15:15–17: "I'm no longer calling you servants because servants don't understand what their master is thinking and planning. No, I've named you friends because I've let you in on everything I've heard from the Father. You didn't choose me, remember; I chose you, and put you in the world to bear fruit, fruit that won't spoil. As fruit bearers, whatever you ask the Father in relation to me, he gives you. But remember the root command: Love one another" (MSG).

Let me put in my words the incredible, almost unbelievable, message God has given us in this amazing passage. God is saying to us, "I appointed you to produce lasting fruit (new Christians) so that whatever you ask for in My name, I will give it to you." In the simplest of terms, the entirety of life is about God loving us ("salvationing" us) into heaven and our loving (allowing God to "salvation" through us) those around us into heaven. Through God's eyes, this is what life on earth is all about.

In Jeremiah 1:5, God explains it more fully: "Before I formed you in the womb I knew you, and before you were born I consecrated you" (ESV). Requiring you to share your faith was not an afterthought. It's why He made you! But winning the lost was not His primary reason. In Isaiah 43:10, God gives this totally amazing explanation of why He made the sharing of your faith His primary role for your life.

I hope you can grasp this! You will spend the rest of your life living in the favor of God if you'll live it understanding what God is telling you in Isaiah 43:10: "You are my witnesses and my servant whom I have chosen, so that you may know and believe me and understand that I am [God]" (CSB).

GRASP THIS!
ISAIAH 43:10

Again, notice that He doesn't say "...so you will know and believe more." It's clear that the intimacy you have with God, when you follow His nudge and He speaks through you to an unbeliever, changes everything! That's when you'll absolutely know and believe and understand that He is God. From that time forward, you'll forever live in the FOG.

This is where the nudge enters the scene. All of us know what the nudge is because it happens continually. The question is, Are you responding? God nudges you to call someone in distress, but you have no idea what to say. You're talking to an unsaved friend, and God nudges you to ask them if you could pray for them, but you don't want to look foolish. You see someone in need, and God nudges you to stop and go back, but you have a schedule to keep.

One of the best things I can offer you, as a lifetime follower of Christ, is decades of experience. And I can honestly tell you that every time I've followed God's nudge, I've been thankful. It often scares me to think of what could have happened if I hadn't followed God's nudge on many occasions. Which leads me to wonder, how many times have I ignored His nudge and let Him down?

Let me finish this chapter by explaining what it's like to live in the FOG. It has nothing to do with any goodness or accomplishments in our lives. The dictionary defines friendship as a state of mutual affection, esteem, intimacy, and trust. It's a two-sided relationship with both sides doing their part. Karen and I are blessed with a circle of friends who have been there for each other for over fifty years. Equally so, our friendship with God is two-sided with our loving Him, living our lives for His purpose, and God allowing us into His family and giving us His incredible gift of eternal life. We come out ahead on that one—a million times over!

THE ECSTASY OF REAL FREEDOM

Like most of you, we have an abundance of secular friends who can't imagine giving up their freedom to a holy God. In their perception, it would be the end of life as they know it. And that, of course, is true. The baggage in their life would be gone. What they don't understand is the ecstasy of real freedom, knowing there's no longer any separation between them and God, having no fear because God has their back, having their days filled with joy and a life that's beyond anything they could have ever imagined. Who doesn't want that?

At eighty years of age, Karen and I have never had more energy or more fun, knowing God is directing our steps. If I die tomorrow, it's going to be with a smile on my face. There's no freedom that rivals knowing nothing can happen to us unless He's in it and can use it for His glory.

Wherever we go is our mission field. Whether we're walking down the street, shopping in the mall, eating at a restaurant, or sitting in a waiting room, we understand that more than 80 percent of the people around us are lost and searching for God. How are they going to know God loves them unless someone tells them? That's our job! But we can't talk with everyone, and not everyone is ready to talk. That's why we're always on the ready for God's nudges (1 Pet. 3:15). It's a partnership!

That's our side of our two-sided friendship with God. Jesus said if we love Him, we will keep His commandments. And then He explained that the two greatest commandments are loving Him and loving our neighbors as ourselves—being as concerned for their salvation as we are our own. And there's zero pressure. He does all the work. He gives you the nudge to start the conversations, and He gives you the words to say.

Karen and I were at a car rally and stopped in Savannah, Georgia, for the night. After dinner I walked to a store that I noticed when we drove in. She wanted some snacks for the next day. It was a moonless night, and there were no streetlights, but I managed to find the little neighborhood store. It was charming, and I was enjoying the experience of being this old white guy, the only white guy in the store. They were so kind.

When I got in line at the register, I noticed a young mom in front of me with all her kid-oriented snacks and cereals. Shortly after she got to the register, she discovered she didn't have enough money to pay for her groceries. It was very awkward for her, and she was embarrassed. The cashier set her groceries to the side while she went outside to call someone for money. With the nudge, I told the cashier to add her groceries to my bill. When I walked outside and found her on the phone, I whispered to her that her groceries were paid for.

She quickly ended her call and asked how that was possible. I said, "I was behind you in line, and when I saw what happened, God told me to pay for your groceries and then tell you He loves you." Before I knew it, she was sobbing on my chest, saying, "I know He does, I know He does." There we were, an old white guy and a young black mom, holding each other outside of a neighborhood grocery store, knowing that was a God moment for both of us. There was no separation between us, nor should there ever be for any of us. Forget the exterior; God looks at our hearts.

We're fishers of men, so I'm continually throwing out bait in every direction to let people know I'm a Christian. Again, it's like sport, always thinking of ways to inject God into our normal conversations, without raising eyebrows—praying they'll take the bait and start asking questions.

This is when your Bible study and prayer life explodes with purpose. In fact, everything in your life has purpose once you're in the game. Now you understand that everything you say and do is leading everyone watching you closer or further away from God. You'll never again view your prayer life and Bible study as obligations. Sharing your faith drives you to your knees and into the Word with energy, joy, and anticipation. You can't wait to get there! This is how sharing your faith builds your faith and makes everything else in your life look pale in comparison.

This is what living in the FOG looks like, with God making everything in your life work for good. When things go wrong, you know God's up to something. There's a ministry opportunity brewing! You just have to look for it. That's when worry is replaced with the wonder of God and total, complete freedom. There's nothing like knowing nothing can hurt you unless God is going to use it for His glory!

That's living in the FOG.

SCRIPTURES FOR DEEPER REFLECTION

- **Being good doesn't get you or anyone else into heaven:** Ephesians 2:8 (NIV)

- **You can't earn your way into heaven:** John 14:6 (NIV)

- **We're like filthy rags compared to the pureness of our holy God:** Isaiah 64:6 (NIV)

- **All of us are in the same boat—needing a Savior:** Romans 3:10 (NKJV)

- **God never leaves you when you love and serve Him:** Hebrews 13:5 (ESV)

- **God is with us, His disciples, to the end:** Matthew 28:20 (NLT)

- **God loves you as much as He's ever loved anyone— even His Son, Jesus Christ:** Psalm 139:17–18 (NLT)

- **The God who created everything in existence wants to be your friend:** John 15:15–17 (MSG)

- **God set you apart to be His spokesperson before you were born:** Jeremiah 1:5 (ESV)

- **Sharing your faith is secondarily about winning the lost and primarily about igniting you!** Isaiah 43:10 (NIV)

- **Always be ready for God to nudge you into a conversation:** 1 Peter 3:15 (NIV)

CHAPTER 18

NO COINCIDENCES!

WE WERE OUT of town and running late for dinner with a friend who always wants to get there first to give his credit card to the waiter. I couldn't let that happen, but my rideshare app wasn't working. So I told Karen we needed to get outside the front door of the hotel so my app would work. But it still didn't work.

That's when Karen suggested I grab the cab in front of us. So I said to the guy, "We'll take that cab." But he said, "Sorry, sir, that cab is taken." Say what? "Taken by who?" He said, "By the lady standing behind you by the front of the hotel." When I asked how long it would take to get another cab, he said, "Well, it's five o'clock so it could take fifteen minutes." That's when the blood started flowing from my head.

At that point I heard a lady saying, "Sir?" I looked around, and it was the lady whose cab I wanted. She said, "Go ahead and take that cab. My husband is still upstairs. I don't know what he's doing. We'll take the next cab." We were so excited over getting this cab. We thanked her and ran to the cab, only to hear the driver yelling profanities as we climbed in.

Once we were in, he asked where we wanted to go as he continued his profanities nonstop. And then we were off with a jerk and screeching tires. What had we gotten ourselves into? Turned out his wife had just died from a long bout with cancer, and his kids were now completely out of control and in rebellion.

A normal passenger would have wanted to escape from that cab at the first stop. But I was waiting for God to tell me what to say, and it came fast. I said, "Sir, God's Word tells us what to do when we're upset. He says, 'Come to me, all you who are weary and burdened, and I will give you rest'" (Matt. 11:28). And he yelled with the same intensity of his obscenities, "Boy, do I need rest!" At that point I knew we had his attention and that this was a divine appointment.

God gave us continuous scriptures, one after another, for the entire trip to the restaurant, and he kept saying, "Yes, that's what I need. That's exactly what I need. I need God. I need to get back in church!" When we got to the restaurant, all three of us got out of the cab, I paid him, and then I said, "If you will trust me with your cell number, I'll find a good church close to you and text you the name and address." He couldn't say yes fast enough.

We offered to pray for him, and he couldn't say yes fast enough again. So there we were, with people walking by us into the restaurant, seeing Karen and me praying with arms around each other in a circle with the taxi driver in front of his headlights. We laughed later, wondering what that must have looked like to people walking by us into the restaurant and the conversations it must have sparked. For sure, it was life changing for that cab driver.

There are no coincidences! Think of all that God had to do to orchestrate that divine appointment. There's no question that God directs our steps and the steps of those He wants us to move closer to Him. First of all, He had to stop my rideshare app from working. Then He had to keep the lady's husband upstairs long enough to have her take the next taxi. Then He had to have that exact taxi driver at my hotel at the right moment.

Once you have extraordinary events like this happening on a regular basis, you know they're not coincidences. They're divine appointments. And every time you have one, it explodes your faith and you can't wait for the next one.

I was waiting for a delayed flight at the Dallas/Fort Worth airport. We were two hours late, the waiting room was packed, and the lady at the podium began calling names of standbys who didn't answer. At that point a disheveled young man dressed in army fatigue shorts and a T-shirt started yelling at her across the waiting area, "Stop calling those names. We're two hours late, and they're all gone. Let's board!"

I immediately turned to my ministry team, who was traveling

with me, and told them, "That's my seatmate!" He boarded before me, and sure enough, when I looked down the aisle, he was seated in the seat next to mine. It was not a coincidence. I broke out laughing and said, "OK, Lord, I'm going in!"

When I crossed over him to sit down, I acted naïve and asked him, "Well, how are you doing today?" He immediately said, "I'm having a horrible day. I just left my firstborn daughter off at college. We've never been apart, and it's tearing me up inside."

I said, "Boy, I know all about that. After we took Michelle, our firstborn daughter, to college and left her, I couldn't speak for the next ten hours. Every time I tried to speak, I broke down crying."

He asked how I got through it, and I started quoting scriptures that he already knew. Sometimes he completed the scripture for me. So I said, "You're obviously a Christian as well." And he explained that he had grown up in church, his dad was a pastor, but he hadn't gone to church or talked to his dad in years.

At this point God was giving me scriptures and illustrations and truth that became like body blows in a heavyweight fight—to which he finally said in an outburst, "I think God put you in this seat beside me!" And I laughed and said, "Did you just figure that out?"

We prayed together as we landed, with his focus completely changed. I could have been mad at God for sitting me next to this lunatic. But this time God let me know before it happened what was going to happen. And my faith exploded!

THE SAME YESTERDAY, TODAY, AND FOREVER

It's true that our circumstances today are decidedly different from those in the time of the apostles, but God is the same yesterday, today, and forever (Heb. 13:8). He works on us and through us just as He did with the apostle Paul. Paul went through every kind of bad imaginable, including beatings, shipwrecks, and imprisonment, and yet he told us in Romans 8:18: "I consider that our present sufferings are not worth comparing with the glory that will be revealed in us."

I spoke to my dear friend Reuben right after the memorial service for his second wife, who had died from cancer. Reuben is one of the godliest men in my life. I was upset and told him I was going to have to ask God about this one. He quickly said to me, "You know, Barry, I thought about that. You know what the bummer is? The bummer is that when I see Him face-to-face, I won't remember the question." That was profound! He had obviously already thought that one through. All our *why* questions will be meaningless in heaven!

SHIPWRECKS AND SNAKEBITES

Paul was the one who penned the words, as God inspired him, that all things work together for good when we love Him and live for His purpose. He understood how God is always at work in our adversities either to perfect us or to open doors for ministry. Most people come to God during adversity, and oftentimes we need to share in their adversities to reach them, with reactions far different from theirs.

Remember how God allowed Paul to be shipwrecked on his way to Rome, as a prisoner, to speak before Caesar? Paul could have easily said, "Really, God? Where are You when I need You?" But Paul already knew that when bad things happen, God is up to something! It wasn't a coincidence that they were just off the shores of Malta.

I suspect Paul asked God curiously, "What are You up to now?" We find this story in Acts 28. He ended up being stranded for three months on Malta, and God gave him favor with the people, loving on them, healing the sick, and telling them about Jesus. How else could God have reached the natives of Malta with the good news of the gospel?

I'm always struck by how even the bite of a poisonous snake didn't distract Paul or have any effect on him while he was in the middle of doing what God wanted him to do. To be honest, that's why I never fear germs or anything else when I know I'm doing exactly what God wants me to do. Not when I'm living in the FOG.

Then there was the time when Paul found himself in prison and penned this great perspective in Philippians 1:12–13: "Now I want you to know, brethren, that my circumstances have turned out for the greater progress of the gospel, so that my imprisonment in the cause of Christ has become well known throughout the whole praetorian guard and to everyone else" (NASB). The Praetorian Guard were the personal bodyguards and intelligence agents for the Roman emperors. Figure that! Some of the most influential men in the Roman Empire were given the good news because Paul was put in prison. And who knows how many people they influenced? Coincidence?

Have you ever found yourself with a flat tire or in an accident, only to discover that there was no other way you could have had that conversation about God with someone you never would have met otherwise? Or did you miss that opportunity?

We recently purchased a home in Arizona and did a complete remodel. We ended up with Annette as our decorator, and she's the best on the planet. She's been a gift from God, and she's led us closer to Jesus. We prayed over every decision, knowing the house was going to be an event center for ministry events.

As happy as ever, she called me the day before Christmas Eve to tell me she would not be able to meet on Friday as planned. I said, "No worries, it's Christmas. Enjoy yourself." She said, "Well, it's a little more than that. I'm in the hospital." I could not have been more shocked. Turned out she had broken her femur in a freak misstep, and she was going to be operated on the next day, Christmas Eve. I never would have known it by her happy demeanor.

I immediately said, "God is in this. He doesn't make mistakes. He's up to something." She agreed, and we bantered and acknowledged the obvious: no one wants to be in the hospital on Christmas, which led us to the conclusion that God wanted her to be a light in the darkness of that hospital. She would have been that anyway because that's who she is. But my words gave her added purpose.

She had a miraculous recovery, with so many stories coming out of that experience. But one was more than impressive. In February, as we were walking down the aisles looking at slabs of marble, she took a phone call and stepped aside. It was a long and laugh-filled conversation. When Annette returned to us, she spontaneously said, "I'm so thankful I was in the hospital for Christmas." Her call came from a girl she had led to the Lord while she was in the hospital.

It was not a coincidence that Annette and this nurse both ended up where they never wanted to be on Christmas Day. There's a famous phrase that says, "When you least expect it, expect it." When things are making you the most unhappy, look around!

Have you noticed how often bad things happen "coincidentally"? One thing after another builds up to where they can be overwhelming. It's never a coincidence that these things are happening to you all at once. Nothing happens unless God allows it or ordains it. God is always up to something! It's your job to figure out what it is. It may just be letting your joy and peace and love shine through the darkness of your situation, which leads someone to Jesus. If one soul comes to the Lord because of your pain, it's worth it.

Karen and I flew to Chicago to change planes to go to Manchester, New Hampshire, for a car rally hosted by Richie and Sharon Clyne. But our forty-five-minute layover turned into a two-and-a-half-hour delay, which made us the last plane to land at the Manchester airport that night. The airport was empty, our baggage carousel was the last one moving, and our two bags were the last to come off, after a delay. Everyone else was gone. Then we walked out the doors to discover that the driver who was supposed to meet us was nowhere in sight. When I called our car service, I was told they couldn't find our driver and didn't know how to get a driver because it was one o'clock in the morning.

At that moment an announcement came over the PA that the airport was now closed. We looked back, and the lights were off. We looked around, and not a single car or individual was in sight. We were completely alone, and our hotel was an hour's drive from us. My assistant, Cathie, who's never failed me in forty years, was beside herself trying to find a driver for us, and Karen and I just laughed. I pointed to two benches and told Karen, "At least there's a bench for each of us. Whenever things go wrong, we know God is up to something, and it's going to be fine." So we talked about how this had to be happening so we could talk to someone who needed Jesus. I suspect anyone else would have been in panic.

In about fifteen minutes, Cathie located a driver who took a passenger to Boston that night and was dead-heading back. Once we were in his car, heading for our hotel, he asked, "What was going through your minds, standing there all alone?"

I said, "You really want to know?" And he said yes. I told him we decided that there must be someone God wanted us to talk to that night about Jesus. And he said, "That's amazing. I've been going through a rough stretch and decided I need to get back in church and talk to someone about God."

God is so good! We spent the next hour talking about God, sharing scriptures, and getting him back on track. When we arrived at the hotel, we locked arms and prayed together like it was the middle of the day. It was 3:00 a.m. when we crawled into bed wide awake and talking nonstop about what just happened. Without God, this would have been a "nightmare from hell" story. But with God, it was a miraculous evening that we'll never forget!

So what did we learn from this? From the delay at Chicago O'Hare, to the last bags off the carousel, to our lost driver, to finding this driver, who was searching for God, dead-heading back from Boston at one o'clock in the morning...

There are no coincidences!

SCRIPTURES FOR DEEPER REFLECTION

- **A great scripture for those whose lives are out of control:** Matthew 11:28 (NIV)

- **God is the only thing in the universe that never changes:** Hebrews 13:8 (NIV)

- **We're defined by how we react to the problems we face:** Romans 8:18 (NIV)

- **When things go wrong, God is up to something:** Acts 28:1–10 (NIV)

- **There are no coincidences:** Philippians 1:12–13 (KJV)

CHAPTER 19

ARE YOU CHANGING YOUR ENVIRONMENT?

It's PAST TIME to take personal responsibility for the world you're living in. There's no question that most of us can't change the world. But you can change your world. And if all of us change *our* worlds, we'll change the world.

Remember, over 80 percent of the unchurched are hoping there's a God who can end the chaos, are looking for someone to tell them, and already have at least one Christian in their life that they trust. We could ignite America with revival in thirty days!

WE COULD IGNITE AMERICA!

Some Christians have more influence than others, but we all have influence. The question is, What are you doing with the influence God has given you? Are you using it for things that will be meaningless in one hundred years, or on the one thing you can celebrate for eternity? For Christians, the only thing that will matter a hundred years from now is how many people are in heaven because of our influence.

Years ago Karen and I had the most amazing travel experience of our lives following the footsteps of Paul on a three-masted sailing ship called *The Sea Cloud*. Our leaders were Bob Coley and Russ Spittler, the top two New Testament scholars in the Assemblies of God. Our voyage took us from the Isle of Patmos to Philippi to Turkey and the sites of the seven churches of Revelation. We toured in the coolness of the mornings, followed by on-deck lectures in the afternoons while we were under sail. It was an incredible experience.

During that trip I met Naomi Dowdy, a missionary pastor in Singapore who's still going strong today. She's one of the most amazing ministers of God I've ever met. I couldn't listen fast enough to capture all the godly wisdom that flowed out of this incredible lady. It was a moment in time when I was in the limited space of a boat with her for a week.

One of her most profound comments was also one of the simplest. We were talking about influence and how we can change the world, not just as denominations and churches, but as individuals. This brought us to the subject of being salt and light. She pointed out that salt and light only have one characteristic in common: they both change their environment.

Then she said every Christian can be defined by this question: Are you changing your environment, or is it changing you? Whoa! That cuts to the chase immediately. The question being asked is, Are you moving your environment closer to God, or is your environment moving you further away from God? You need to ask yourself that question.

Unfortunately, the next question is far easier to answer: Is the church moving our environment closer to God, or is our environment moving the church further away from God? With only 51 percent of our pastors still holding a biblical worldview, and less than 10 percent of our sermons even mentioning salvation, there's no question that our environment has changed our churches. Most of our churches have remained silent, refusing to use their influence, while godless politicians are systematically removing all traces of God from our national mindset.

Those with convictions are willing to die for them. We're seeing that today wherever Christians are being persecuted. But the destruction to our way of life in America is being destroyed with equal vengeance as we sit and watch. We're like the proverbial frog in cool water, gradually increased to boiling water, and doing nothing. Our environment is changing us while we do nothing.

Without question, our problems are spiritual, and they can't be solved with the minds of man, politically or racially. That's an exercise in futility. We're in spiritual warfare, with Satan being the god of this world (2 Cor. 4:4) blinding the eyes of so much of our population and causing them to see evil as good and good as evil. This explains how educated adults can favor insanity like giving explicit sex information and puberty blockers to grade school kids without their parents' knowledge.

Thank God for dedicated Christians who are putting themselves, and their families, on the line to serve in public office today. And shame on those pastors who spoke so strongly against Christians being in public office, and in the press and media, and in the entertainment industries. We handed all those places of influence over to godless people who are now using them to abolish everything that's Christian and God-honoring in America.

Most of us can't fight those battles on a personal basis. But you can fight them at the ballot box, using the Bible as your voting guide. With God's help, you need to critically judge every candidate by what they've actually done, not by what they say. This is part of your stewardship to the Lord.

It can easily be argued that the most patriotic thing you can do for America is to move everyone, every day, closer to Jesus. Never debate or argue with anyone. People can't see truth with blinded eyes. Proverbs 26:4 tells us: "Don't answer the foolish arguments of fools, or you will become as foolish as they are" (NLT). Matthew 7:6 says it even better: "Don't waste what is holy on people who are unholy. Don't throw your pearls to pigs! They will trample the pearls, then turn and attack you" (NLT).

It's only when unbelievers come to Jesus that God can restore their ability to see the truth. Only then will they have the discernment to vote for those who will honor God and save America. In all seriousness, God is the only answer for spiritual blindness. Being a missionary for God is being a missionary for America.

What is it that holds the greatest importance in your life? Are you able to see beyond whatever you're enjoying today that will soon end, to see what you can be enjoying when eternity has begun? Your level of spiritual maturity is revealed by how you answer this question. Psalm 103:15–17 says it well: "Our days on earth are like grass; like wildflowers, we bloom and die. The wind blows, and we are gone—as though we had never been here. But the love of the LORD remains forever with those who fear him" (NLT).

The Lord wants you to enjoy to the fullest everything He's placed in your hands, as long as those things don't replace God as your first love. When God is your first love, it's obvious to everyone. I gravitate to "first love" Christians wherever I find them. One of my wife's best college friends married a "first love" guy in the latter years of her life. He was older than me, with a bit of country in him and not well-spoken, but so close to God I couldn't get enough of him. When he came into the room, I ran to Bob and always sat next to him, wanting to have more of what he had. Everywhere Bob went, he changed his environment. That's the kind of people we want to be and hang out with.

Second Corinthians 2:15–16 says: "For we are the aroma of Christ to God among those who are being saved and among those who are perishing, to one a fragrance from death to death, to the other a fragrance from life to life" (ESV). For me, Bob brought a life-to-life fragrance into my life. But for those rejecting God, people like Bob bring conviction and the remembrance that there's a finality to this life. The same Spirit that brings truth and celebration brings conviction and guilt and even rejection.

One day I was sitting on Balboa Island watching the boats go by. I noticed a tiny boat with a tiny outboard engine making lots of noise going slowly down the bay. The bow of the boat was up high, with the driver at the rear steering the boat while leaning forward in an attempt to gain speed. It brought back memories of my childhood adventures with my own 2.5 horsepower Elgin engine-powered rowboat.

Then I noticed how after that tiny little boat went by its tiny little wake was still moving every boat and dock. Even the big boats were responding to the tiny wake from that little boat. And it hit me! Wherever we go, we should leave a wake…a ripple effect…an aroma of a Christ-follower having been in that room, with every perception we leave behind honoring God and moving people closer to Jesus. Just the presence of the Holy Spirit in our lives should change our environments.

As a Christian, you're the light on the hill when you let it shine, that's easily noticed and immediately attractive in the darkness of this world. People are desperate for what we have. They're searching for light in the darkness. And yet most Christians are allowing their environment to cause them to hide their light either on purpose or without thinking. It never enters their mind that they're letting God down.

I was in a restaurant for lunch with a friend who ate there several times a week with the same server. When I asked if he knew whether she was a Christian, he said, "I don't know." Then he asked me how to do that without making a scene. I said, "When you introduced me just now, you could have easily said I'm a friend from your church, which would have immediately told her that you're a Christian and started your opportunity to lead her to Jesus." It was a brand-new thought to him. This is how you change your environment everywhere you go. Immediately find a way to identify yourself as a Christian without raising an eyebrow, and then start chumming—throwing out tasty tidbits that make them hungry for God.

It's so wrong and so widely believed that actions by themselves speak louder than words, as if being a good customer and a good tipper has anything to do with God. At the same time, when you do those things you have the influence to change people's lives. This adds purpose to your good works, even to the smallest things you do in life.

The world views influence as the currency to gain favor for self-interests. For those of us whose eyes are fixed on the Lord, the far larger goal is to use the influence God gives us to lead people to Him. When we accept Jesus Christ as the Lord of our lives, we literally dedicate our lives to Him and want to live our lives for His purpose. It's interesting how Paul uses the term *bondservant* to describe how we choose to serve God, because our lives are far better serving God than serving ourselves.

When we serve God, He makes our lives better. In Matthew 25:23, Jesus says: "Well done, you good and faithful servant. You have been faithful over a few things. I will make you ruler over many things. Enter the joy of your master" (MEV). When we're faithful to God in the smallest of things, God takes us to the next level. When there's consistency in our walk over time, in increasing levels, God gives us the influence to change our environment. You can liken serving God to running a marathon.

I started this chapter with a reminder that all of us have influence. How you use your influence changes your environment for good or evil. Are you moving people closer or further away from Jesus? Do your actions match your words when you're talking about God? Are you aware of and do you care about the spiritual condition of those around you? Do you want to be part of the cause or part of the solution to the problems that are tearing America apart?

SATAN IS HAVING A FIELD DAY

Satan is having a field day right now, with most of the world following his lead. He's taking my breath away by the power he's exhibiting all over the world at the same time. I've gone so far as to tell him he's far more powerful than I realized. I'm impressed, and most of the world is following his lead.

For those of you who are in corporate America or politics or entertainment or education or even ministry (pastors), it's more than tempting to play to your financial supporters or your fans or your congregations by giving place to Satan (Eph. 4:27), allowing him to push you back from what you once knew was truth. That's what is happening wholesale worldwide. Championing Satan's causes is the easiest way to get ahead in this world for all the wrong reasons at the worst possible time in human history.

With almost 80 percent of our population being unchurched and less than 6 percent of our population still holding to a biblical worldview, we're in the worst-case scenario for the trumpet to sound with the voice of the archangel. That's when those who have accepted Jesus Christ as their Lord and Savior will be called up to meet Him (1 Thess. 4:16) in the air to be with Him forevermore. It's called the rapture of the church, and it could happen at any time. Matthew 24:37–39 describes it well: "When the Son of Man returns, it will be like it was in Noah's day. In those days before the flood, the people were enjoying banquets and parties and weddings right up to the time Noah entered his boat. People didn't realize what was going to happen until the flood came and swept them all away. That is the way it will be when the Son of Man comes" (NLT).

The gravity of our current situation and the clarity of Scripture collide in Matthew 7:13–14: "You can enter God's Kingdom only through the narrow gate. The highway to hell is broad, and its gate is wide for the many who choose that way. But the gateway to life is very narrow and the road is difficult, and only a few ever find it" (NLT).

Are you taking the broad path, going with the flow and doing nothing to change what's happening? The failure of the church, and most Christians, to use their influence to change our environment is what got us here. We, the church, have allowed the destruction of America—and hundreds of millions of souls—by failing to use the influence God gave us to change our environment.

This is not a political issue. The only way to change our environment is to ignite Christians to ignite America with revival, one person at a time.

SCRIPTURES FOR DEEPER REFLECTION

- **Most Americans are lost, blinded, and unable to see the light:** 2 Corinthians 4:4 (NIV)

- **Avoid arguments like the plague:** Proverbs 26:4 (NLT)

- **Avoid those who want a debate more than answers:** Matthew 7:6 (NLT)

- **Are you able to see beyond whatever you're enjoying today?** Psalm 103:15–16 (NLT)

- **The same Spirit that brings truth and celebration brings conviction:** 2 Corinthians 2:15–16 (ESV)

- **When we're faithful, God takes us to the next level:** Matthew 25:23 (MEV)

- **Every time you pull back from serving God, Satan fills the space:** Ephesians 4:26–27 (ESV)

- **The rapture is a real event that can happen at any moment:** 1 Thessalonians 4:16 (NKJV)

- **When you least expect it, expect it!** Matthew 24:37–39 (NLT)

- **America's Godlessness is about to collide with God's judgment:** Matthew 7:13–14 (NLT)

CHAPTER 20

BEING GOOD ISN'T GOOD ENOUGH

"**B**EING GOOD ISN'T good enough" is one of the most repeated messages throughout this book. But it's such an overwhelming error that permeates the church that even a full chapter on this subject may not kill it!

Believing that being good gets you into heaven contradicts all logic and the entire reason why God sent His only Son to suffer the agony of the cross. Why would God want His Son to become a man and suffer the most inhumane, excruciatingly painful method of killing ever devised by humans? There's only one reason Jesus would make Himself man, dwell among us, and sacrifice His life. It's the only way He could justify allowing us, as sinful man, to enter into the holy presence of almighty God.

An abundance of scriptures describe the absurdity of our good compared to God's holiness. Jeremiah 17:9 tells us what we already know: "The heart is deceitful above all things, and desperately wicked: who can know it?" (KJV).

Who can comprehend the mind of God, who is and was and always will be? He's the One who created everything in existence, permeating endlessly beyond what our telescopes can even see 50 billion light-years away, while being with you right now as you read this book. God lacks nothing, and yet He created us to rule with Him over the angels for eternity. It's impossible for our finite minds to fully grasp what He's offered us. Why is it so hard for us to accept God's gift of eternal life?

But it's our decision to make! God has given us the power to decide for ourselves where we want to spend eternity. One of our clearest understandings from birth is rewards and punishments. We don't have to teach our toddlers to steal cookies and tell them it's wrong and that they'll get punished if caught. They already know that. As our kids get older, the rewards and punishments get larger because the stakes are higher.

With rewards and punishments being one of our most basic instincts, God made the logic behind heaven and hell abundantly clear and easy to understand—the ultimate form of rewards and punishments. "It is appointed unto men once to die, but after this the judgment" (Heb. 9:27, KJV).

It's important to point out that God doesn't want to send anyone to hell—and indeed He doesn't. Second Peter 3:9–10 (NLT) puts it in perspective:

> [God] is being patient for your sake. He does not want anyone to be destroyed, but wants everyone to repent. But the day of the Lord will come as unexpectedly as a thief. Then the heavens will pass away with a terrible noise, and the very elements themselves will disappear in fire, and the earth and everything on it will be found to deserve judgment.

There's only one thing God can't do. He can't make us love Him. That's because He has given us free choice, and He won't go back on His Word. It would not give God any pleasure to be surrounded by those He programmed to love Him. It's your choice and your choice alone if you want to love God, live for His purpose, and receive His gift of eternal life

ONE THING GOD CAN'T DO

or live according to your own rules, reject His offer, and spend eternity in hell. It's your choice.

The superlatives of heaven and horrors of hell are graphically described in the Scriptures and leave no ambiguity over their both being real places. Deciding not to accept Jesus Christ as your Savior and Lord, or making no decision at all, amounts to the same thing. Make no mistake! The decision on where you're going to spend your eternity is the most important decision of your life.

Regardless of all the cartoons of the red devil with his pitchfork and partying forever with your "good" friends, hell is a very real place reserved for the devil. Here's the problem: if you refuse or fail to accept Jesus Christ as your Savior and Lord, your sinfulness will be what sends you to hell. Jesus Himself said in John 3:3: "I tell you the truth, unless you are born again, you cannot see the Kingdom of God" (NLT). When your sinfulness prevents your entrance into heaven, there's only one other place to go.

Proverbs 14:12 tells us: "There is a way which seemeth right unto a man, but the end thereof are the ways of death" (KJV). My greatest heartbreak is for my unsaved friends who foolishly believe that God would never send them to hell after all the good things they've done in their lives. But God doesn't send anyone to hell. There's nowhere else to go when the doors to heaven are closed to you (Matt. 25).

I spoke earlier of how God's love is salvation. When He loves us, He's "salvationing" us. First Corinthians 13:1–3 makes it abundantly clear that doing good things for the sole purpose of being good has nothing to do with God's plan for mankind:

> If I speak in the tongues of men or of angels, but do not have love, I am only a resounding gong or a clanging cymbal. If I have the gift of prophecy and can fathom all mysteries and all knowledge, and if I have a faith that can move mountains, but do not have love, I am nothing. If I give all I possess to the poor and give over my body to hardship that I may boast, but do not have love, I gain nothing.

In simple terms, you can feel good, even proud, about helping those who are less fortunate. Feeding and clothing the poor is a righteous act of kindness. But if you do all that and have not love, if you're not allowing God to use your goodness to "salvation" the less fortunate, you gain nothing. You're like a *resounding gong* or *clanging cymbal*.

The life of a Christian is not about helping others to have more fun or be better dressed and better fed on their way to hell. How empty and shallow are those thoughts? Our lives are about doing all that and more, with the added bonus of using every resource God gives us to love them, to "salvation" them into heaven.

Every people group, from the beginning of time, has attempted to reconcile themselves to their perception of God with the shedding of blood. They threw babies and virgins into volcanoes and cut themselves violently. The children of Israel were directed by God to sacrifice a lamb without blemish. Their sacrifices in the temple were a precursor to Christ, the Lamb of God, who sacrificed His sinless life for all of us. He suffered and died the agony of the cross to pay the price for all our sins.

There is a difference between being a good person with a sinful nature that separates you from God and being seen by God as righteous and justified to enter into His presence. Listen to how Isaiah describes this moment: "I am overwhelmed with joy in the LORD my God! For he has dressed me with the clothing of salvation and draped me in a robe of righteousness. I am like a bridegroom dressed for his wedding or a bride with her jewels" (Isa. 61:10, NLT). If you have yet to experience this moment in your life, please go to SeekingGod.org right now and secure your eternity.

I'm guessing you've never heard a message on evangelism that likens it to sport. But even God gave reference to it in Hebrews 12:1: "Therefore, since we are surrounded by such a great cloud of witnesses, let us throw off everything that hinders and the sin that so easily entangles. And let us run with perseverance the race marked out for us." Indeed, it is a race! And we should be running flat-out for our entire lives.

You've been reconciled to God by the forgiveness of your sins. And from now until your last breath, that's your full-time ministry. Second Corinthians 5:18 explains it well: "God, who hath reconciled us to himself by Jesus Christ...hath given to us the ministry of reconciliation" (KJV). Living for God's purpose is literally reconciling those around us to God through Jesus Christ. And we're bound to do that because that's what He did for us!

THE ROADBLOCK

The unbelievable roadblock to this is that less than 10 percent of our sermons today even mention salvation, let alone the Great Commission. Our churches are full of people believing personal goodness is sharing their faith, because three-point "feel good" sermons have become the norm. The role of the pastor to *equip us* (Eph. 4:12) has been lost in the wokeness of our day. It's time to take personal responsibility for the plan God has ordained for you from the time He placed you in your mother's womb (Jer. 1:5).

When you're an ambassador of the United States in a foreign country, everything you do and say, from speaking to Parliament to playing tennis, represents the United States. When you're Christ's ambassador to this world that is now foreign to us, everything you do and say represents God. Second Corinthians 5:20 says: "So we are Christ's ambassadors; God is making his appeal through us. We speak for Christ" (NLT).

Can you grasp the significance of "speaking for Christ"? You're speaking for God? Seriously? God is making His appeal to the lost 80 percent of our population in America through us! Obviously, there's no greater task before us. And if you're a Christian, it's not a matter of choice. No matter where you go in Scripture, you can't get away from the fact that you're representing God and people are forming their opinions about God with everything you do and say. You can't sign up, and you can't opt out.

As Christ's ambassador, being good is not good enough!

SCRIPTURES FOR DEEPER REFLECTION

- **From birth, our inclination is to do the wrong things:** Jeremiah 17:9 (NKJV)

- **All of us will eventually stand alone before God to be judged:** Hebrews 9:27 (NKJV)

- **God's patience is running out:** 2 Peter 3:9–10 (NLT)

- **Not just knowing Jesus but accepting Him as Lord and Savior is your access pass:** John 3:3 (NLT)

- **Believing you can earn your way into heaven is false doctrine:** Proverbs 14:12 (KJV)

- **Doing good things for the sole purpose of doing good things is worthless:** 1 Corinthians 13:1–3 (NIV)

- **Being seen by God as righteous and justified to enter His presence is overwhelming:** Isaiah 61:10 (NLT)

- **We should run flat-out for God to the finish line until we breathe our last breath:** Hebrews 12:1 (NIV)

- **Move everyone, every day, closer to Jesus:** 2 Corinthians 5:18 (KJV)

- **God chose you to share your faith before you were born:** Ephesians 4:12 (KJV)

- **God chose you to share your faith before you were born:** Jeremiah 1:5 (KJV)

- **All Christians are in full-time ministry:** 2 Corinthians 5:20 (NLT)

CHAPTER 21

THIS IS WAR!

Make no mistake about it, we're engaged in a war. It's an invisible, cosmic conflict that is very real, with very real entities and very real consequences. Ephesians 6:12 describes it well: "For we do not wrestle against flesh and blood, but against principalities, against powers, against the rulers of the darkness of this age, against spiritual hosts of wickedness in the heavenly places" (NKJV).

This has always been a powerful scripture, but now it's over-the-top in describing what's happening across America and around the world today. Indeed, we're seeing unprecedented, unbridled, behind-the-scenes evil manifesting itself in every conceivable area of our lives. From the global to the national and local, and even into our denominations, churches, and families, evil is pervading us and dividing us. Satan is at the top of his game.

With so few Christians reading their Bibles today, and almost none of our pastors even mentioning the existence of Satan or hell, let me inject a brief perspective. We're told in Revelation 12 how Satan and a third of the angels (now demons) were cast out of heaven and now want to take us with them into the pit of hell.

Remember that nothing happens unless God allows it or ordains it to happen. In Job 2:1–4 we learn that Satan couldn't attack Job without God's permission. And in Job 42:10 we learn that Job ended up with twice as much as he had before. It's comforting to know that God will never allow you to be tempted more than you can endure (1 Cor. 10:13). It could be argued that big challenges are a compliment from God because He knows you can handle them and they will grow your faith and testimony.

In fact, if we didn't have trials, we would have no way of building our faith. James 1 tells us to count it all joy when trials come upon us, for that very reason. On a personal basis, I can tell you that facing the immediate loss of my business, being told in ICU that I was dying, and the sudden loss of our forty-nine-year-old daughter provided Karen and me with our greatest spiritual growth spurts.

While the apostle Paul said that Satan is the god of this world (2 Cor. 4:4), it is only at the pleasure of God and His divine plan of perfecting us for eternity. If we were not tempted with the distraction of Satan and his legion of demons, there would be no choice for us to make between good and evil. But God gave us free choice with the power to follow Satan into hell or Jesus into heaven. It's not complicated. God's Grand Plan is for all of us to spend eternity with Him in heaven—that none should be lost! Satan knows he's going to hell, and he wants to take as many of us as possible with him.

Second Corinthians 4:4 tells us: "The god of this age has blinded the minds of unbelievers, so that they cannot see the light of the gospel that displays the glory of Christ, who is the image of God." In the middle of the riots, when a young man was proudly standing on top of a burning police car, it hit me that I could be that guy. I'm an aggressive guy, and if I was raised like him and didn't know there's a God who loves me and has a plan for my life, I could see myself doing the very same thing. Satan would have my ear!

THE GOD OF THIS WORLD BLINDS

For the most part, those who are doing bad things today are not bad people. They're lost people being manipulated by satanic forces. Their eyes have been blinded. They don't know who God is or if He even exists. That's on us! The blame is on us, the church, because we haven't told them. "How can they hear about him unless someone tells them?" (Rom. 10:14, NLT). That's our responsibility.

GOD IS SAYING "WOE"

We were told this time would come in Isaiah 5:20–21: "Woe to those who call evil good, and good evil; who put darkness for light, and light for darkness; who put bitter for sweet, and sweet for bitter!

Woe to those who are wise in their own eyes, and prudent in their own sight!" (NKJV). When God says, "Woe," you know it's serious! This is the perfect explanation for the insane decisions we're seeing being made today on every front.

The existence of Satan and his legion of demons is a fundamental biblical truth. It's critical that you understand Satan's role if you're going to be effective in directing people away from Satan's influence. Apart from biblical truth, it's impossible to understand and explain what's happening today on a global basis. There's a force that's far bigger than any individual or organization. His name is Satan!

Archibald Brown, who was Charles Spurgeon's successor, said, "The existence of the devil is so clearly taught in the Bible that to doubt it is to doubt the Bible itself."[1] The Scriptures are not ambiguous about the existence of Satan. He's there at the beginning in Genesis 3:1, tempting Eve. He's there in the middle in 1 Chronicles 21:1, provoking David to disobediently number Israel. He's there in Revelation 12:9 when he's cast out. Jesus referred to him twenty-five times. Talking to the religious Pharisees, Jesus said, point-blank, "You belong to your father, the devil, and you want to carry out your father's desires. He was a murderer from the beginning, not holding to the truth, for there is no truth in him. When he lies, he speaks his native language, for he is a liar and the father of lies" (John 8:44). That kind of sums it up.

Jesus made it clear that Satan is real as is his plan to destroy us with his legion of demons, formerly angels, who follow his direction. To be sure, Satan is not a metaphor for evil. He is evil. He hates God, he hates God's creation (us), and he hates God's plan for "salvationing" us and taking us to heaven. From the moment of the fall, Satan has tried to thwart God's plan of redemption. He tried to destroy Israel and corrupt the bloodline to keep Jesus from being born. Satan influenced Herod to slaughter all the innocent baby boys in the region in an attempt to kill the baby Jesus. He tempted Jesus in the wilderness to worship him and thus stop His mission. The Bible is filled with scriptures confirming the existence of Satan.

Satan, of course, is no match for God. Jesus finished His purpose for coming, defeated death, and rose again so mankind can be saved. Now Satan wants to stop us from hearing, understanding, and accepting God's amazing plan of salvation. Nothing makes him angrier than the thought of losing you to God and knowing you'll be living with God forever in heaven. There's no mistaking that Satan is determined to make sure that will never happen. You're a high-value target. And every time he distracts you and makes you fall, he's laughing at you.

THIS IS NOT A GAME

The fact is, it's not a contest. There's no competition for what God has prepared for us. But Jesus gives us clear understanding of Satan's intentions in John 10:10: "The thief comes only to steal and kill and destroy: I came that they may have life and have it abundantly." First Peter 5:8 goes on to say: "Be sober, be vigilant; because your adversary the devil walks about like a roaring lion, seeking whom he may devour" (NKJV).

Satan is real, he has an army of demons working in concert with him, and he's playing for keeps. He wants to kill you and all of God's creation. He literally wants to take as many people as possible to hell with him. This is for real! It's not a game.

Satan knows that God's primary method for spreading the good news of the gospel is through us. Romans 10:14–15 confirms: "And how can they hear without someone preaching to them? And how can anyone preach unless they are sent?" This is where Satan is winning his biggest battle. With more than 80 percent of all Christians living in fear at this moment, he's robbing Christians of their faith and ending their ability to share their faith. You can't share what you don't have. And if you don't share your faith, Satan wins!

The thought of allowing Satan to distract me and laugh at me is my biggest incentive to run in the other direction. Before I started sharing my faith, my faith was weak and I was easily distracted. I wanted to honor God with my life, but I lacked the power to do anything more than go through the motions. I was a defeated

Christian, on my way to heaven, but not feeling good about how I was getting there. Perhaps you're at that point right now. If you are, I have good news for you.

I may sound like a broken record, but it's the message of this book. When you love God and live for His purpose, Satan can't touch you unless God allows it, as He did for Job. Satan can mess with me all he wants, and he'll never stop. But every time it makes me stronger, because I know what Satan means for evil God will use for good (Gen. 50:20), and He always does. That's the end of the war!

That's what led Karen and me on our quest to find joy. That led us to sharing our faith, living our lives for God's purpose—to seek and save the lost—and enjoying God's promise to make everything in our lives work for good.

That's how you end worry—living in the favor of God—and overcome spiritual warfare in one step.

SCRIPTURES FOR DEEPER REFLECTION

- **We're in spiritual warfare:** Ephesians 6:10–12 (NKJV)

- **Satan hates God and us and wants to keep us out of heaven:** Revelation 12:9 (NLT)

- **Satan couldn't touch Job without God's permission:** Job 2:6 (NLT)

- **Job was found faithful through Satan's attacks, and God rewarded him mightily:** Job 42:10 (NIV)

- **Big challenges are a compliment from God:** 1 Corinthians 10:13 (NIV)

- **Most people we view as evil are simply lost and blinded by Satan:** 2 Corinthians 4:4 (NIV)

- **The real problem is the failure of Christians to share their faith:** Romans 10:14 (NLT)

- **Insane decisions are made by those blinded and deceived by Satan:** Isaiah 5:20–21 (NKJV)

- **Satan has been our tempter since the Garden of Eden:** Genesis 3:1–7 (NIV)

- **Satan provoked David's disobedience:** 1 Chronicles 21:1–18 (NIV)

- **Satan was thrown out of heaven:** Revelation 12:9 (NIV)

- **When Satan lies, he speaks his native language:** John 8:44 (NIV)

- **Jesus gave us clear understanding of Satan's intentions:** John 10:10 (ESV)

- **To ignore Satan is to be overtaken by him:** 1 Peter 5:8 (NKJV)

- **God honors the few who are proclaiming the good news:** Romans 10:14–15 (NLT)

- **God is ready to turn the bad stuff in your life into good stuff:** Genesis 50:20 (ESV)

CHAPTER 22

ARE YOU REALLY
A BELIEVER?

MATTHEW 7:21–23 CONTAINS some of the most sobering, frightening, and soul-searching scriptures in the Bible. Verse 21 says, "Not everyone who calls out to me, 'Lord! Lord!' will enter the Kingdom of Heaven. Only those who actually do the will of my Father in heaven will enter" (NLT).

You might say, "Wait a minute! Are we adding something here? I thought if I accepted Jesus Christ as my Savior and Lord, I'm in. Now you're saying I have to *do the will of [the] Father* to get in?" And the answer to that is yes and no. No, there are no additional requirements for entering into heaven beyond accepting Jesus Christ as your Savior and Lord. But yes, if you accept Jesus Christ as your Savior and Lord, you're automatically going to tell people.

Telling people that you've become a Christian is the first thing every new born-again believer does when they get saved. Revelation 2:5 calls it the first work. If you believe you've accepted the Lord but haven't told anyone, you're probably still in transition and not there yet. Just keep on going. You'll know it when you get there.

Romans 10:9 spells this out very clearly: "If you openly declare that Jesus is Lord and believe in your heart that God raised him from the dead, you will be saved" (NLT). You don't have to teach anyone who hits their thumb with a hammer to say, "Ouch!" And you don't have to teach new believers how to tell people they're saved. This is the love God/love your neighbor relationship God wants you to maintain for your entire life.

The next two verses in Matthew 7 are the ones most chilling: "On judgment day many will say to me, 'Lord! Lord! We prophesied in your name and cast out demons in your name and performed many miracles in your name.' But I will reply, 'I never knew you. Get away from me, you who break God's laws'" (NLT).

There's no question God is speaking to overachieving church leaders and attenders, highly regarded in their congregations, who are casting out demons and performing miracles. And it also speaks to their congregations who lack the discernment to know the difference between the real and the counterfeit. With only 21 percent of Evangelicals holding a biblical worldview, it's never been easier for charismatic leaders with false doctrines to attract large numbers of people who don't know the difference. Circuses draw crowds!

At times I've been shaken to the core with unguarded comments coming from ministers I've revered from a distance. Some have fallen mightily, some are still going strong, and, judging by this scripture, some are going to be more than surprised come judgment day. "Vengeance is mine; I will repay, saith the Lord" (Rom. 12:19, KJV).

Without discernment, it's easy to respect and emulate people in our churches for all the wrong reasons. People often speak well, organize well, and give well in our churches, with everyone presuming they're saved. One of the most generous and high-profile givers to Christian causes in America died recently. Everyone presumed he was saved, and no one dared ask for fear of losing his support. Thank God a close friend flew across the country just before he died to finally settle that issue.

What if his friend hadn't done that? After giving millions of dollars to Christian causes, he might have heard what God said in Matthew 7:23, "I never knew you: depart from me" (KJV). This should speak volumes to you if you're going through the motions of being a Christian and being respected as a Christian, without being a Christian. God knows your heart!

Dr. James Dobson, my longtime friend, invited Karen and me to go backstage and have dinner with Bill Gaither before one of his stadium concerts. It was one of the great experiences of our lives. This man, who we've followed with passion his entire career (along with his wife, Gloria), was ten times better than we ever dreamed.

His every word exudes passion for God, occasionally mixed with the folksy humor God has given him.

It's amazing how being around real people who are giants of the faith can impact lives for eternity, even in times of fun. I'm the better for having had a fun dinner backstage with Bill Gaither. And I'm blessed for having a large circle of friends around me who lift me up every time I'm with them. Not just having fun but drawing each other closer to the Lord every time we're together. That's the body of Christ functioning as God intended.

My greatest concern is for the 48 percent of our population who call themselves Christians and yet rarely, if ever, go to church. Most polls indicate that 70 percent of our population self-identify as Christians.[1] And in most cases, they're good people who believe in God and Jesus Christ. But in stark contrast, only 22 percent of our population are currently attending church regularly.[2] That means 48 percent of our population (70% - 22% = 48%) self-identify as Christians without having a weekly church experience and with very little Bible knowledge.

While it's possible to be a devoted Christ follower and not go to church, it rarely happens without a health issue or the absence of a good church. Apart from that, it's a key barometer of your spiritual health. When we love someone, we love to spend time with them. When we love God, we love to spend time with Him. That's why we're told in Hebrews 10:25: "And let us not neglect our meeting together, as some people do, but encourage one another, especially now that the day of his return is drawing near" (NLT). Yes! Especially now that *the day of His return is drawing near.*

A word of caution if you fall into this category: God's rules for your entrance into heaven are not based on your goodness or good intentions, or your words that pay Him lip service. John 14:12 explains: "I tell you the truth, anyone who believes in me will do the same works I have done, and even greater works, because I am going to be with the Father" (NLT).

A WORD OF CAUTION

Ephesians 2:8 tells us: "God saved you by his grace when you believed. And you can't take credit for this; it is a gift from God" (NLT). Without question, you can't earn your way into heaven. But if there's no life change, it's not real. James 2:14 will confirm this for you: "What good is it, dear brothers and sisters, if you say you have faith but don't show it by your actions? Can that kind of faith save anyone?" (NLT). If your faith is real, you're bringing those around you to faith.

IT BREAKS MY HEART

Because I'm a car guy and it's a huge community that feels like family, I have a ton of friends across the country who are among the best people on the planet. Without question, they know Jesus Christ is the Son of God. But, of course, so do the demons in hell. James 2:19 tells us: "You say you have faith, for you believe that there is one God. Good for you! Even the demons believe this, and they tremble in terror" (NLT).

Unfortunately my unsaved car guy friends are having so much fun with their friends and cars and car rallies and car shows that going to church and being concerned over where their friends and family will spend eternity is the last thing on their minds. These are exceptionally smart and successful people, completely ignoring their mortality as if their lives will go on forever. They're the personification of 2 Corinthians 4:4: "Satan, who is the god of this world, has blinded the minds of those who don't believe. They are unable to see the glorious light of the Good News" (NLT). And it breaks my heart.

One of the most famous car guys was George Barris, the "King of Kustomizers." He and his brother were among the very first customizers of hot rods back in the '40s. His movie cars included the Munster Koach, General Lee from *The Dukes of Hazzard*, and the Batmobile. I knew him for fifty years, but he would have nothing to do with God until they discovered he had a brain tumor. Only then, knowing he was dying, did God become a lot more important to George, and I led him to the Lord.

His grandson Jared told the story at George's funeral of how he and his mom, Joji, and a nurse met with George for the last time. The nurse asked George, "What are you most thankful for?" And he responded, "That Jesus is here, and He's saving me." This is incredible! After a lifetime of ignoring God, George and I are going to spend eternity together. But here's my heartbreak: I'm losing too many of my old car guy friends who are dying and missing heaven because they were always too busy and having too much fun to think about God.

I visited one of my car guy friends three times as he lay dying in a hospice bed in his living room. Although he told me emphatically that he didn't want to go to hell, he put me off all three times from leading him to the Lord. He was just a prayer away from going to heaven.

On my last visit, he told me he was too busy. I was speechless and asked, "Too busy?" I hadn't noticed, but they had put up a portable big-screen TV in the living room for him to watch from his hospice bed. And he explained that he wanted to watch the Indy 500 time trials to see who would be on the grid on Sunday. He died a few days later, and—unless he accepted the Lord on his own before he died—he'll remember that he's in hell forever because he was more interested in watching the time trials of the Indy 500 than in accepting Jesus Christ as his Savior and Lord. The reality of that thought haunts me.

The most common excuse for not going to church is, "I'm better than those who go to church." And you may be! But as I've said throughout this book, getting into heaven has nothing to do with how good you are and everything to do with what Jesus did for you on the cross. It's for you to choose God or the things of this world to be your god. This is not the time to be anywhere near the line of demarcation between heaven and hell. Joshua 24:15 tells us: "Choose you this day whom ye will serve!" (KJV).

Of even greater concern is the gray area where most Christians are living their lives today. Seminaries, denominations, pastors, and Christians are departing from the truth of God's Word on a wholesale basis. It's called apostasy, and 1 Timothy 4:1 tells us we should not be surprised by it: "Now the Holy Spirit tells us clearly that in the last times some will turn away from the true faith; they will follow deceptive spirits and teachings that come from demons" (NLT).

With only 51 percent of our pastors, 21 percent of Evangelicals, and only 6 percent of our population still holding a biblical world-view, this is not a small problem. Small wonder that more than 80 percent of Americans, including Christians, are living in fear. At the very time when the church should be a beacon of light in the darkness, we're hiding it under the proverbial "bushel basket." (See Matthew 5:14–16.) God cannot be happy with us.

A SPLINTERED CHURCH

Which brings us to what has been called our church community, which is now splintered into a thousand pieces with not only our churches but our denominations being torn apart. With almost half of those calling themselves Evangelicals believing there's more than one way to heaven, I don't even know what the term means anymore.

Pastor Jack Hibbs, senior pastor of Calvary Chapel Chino Hills in Southern California, recently preached a sermon titled "These Are the Times of the Signs." He pointed out that the "signs" the prophets gave us so we would know when we are in the end times are here. So this is what Luke 21:28 is telling us today: "When these things begin to take place, stand up and lift up your heads, because your redemption is drawing near."

But in spite of all that's happening around us that shouts the message that we should be ready for Christ's return, most Christians have been silenced and demoralized. They've allowed their faith to atrophy. Deceiving themselves, they are merely hearers of the Word and not doers (Jas. 1:22). While their light once shined brightly, they've allowed "the cares of this world [COVID/politics], the deceitfulness of riches, and the desires for other things [family, recreation, escape] entering in, choke the word, and it becomes unfruitful" (Mark 4:19, NKJV).

Indeed, there are rewards in heaven for those following God's will and purpose. But 1 Corinthians 3:13–15 offers a warning for those simply going through the motions of being a Christian: "But on the judgment day, fire will reveal what kind of work each builder has done. The fire will show if a person's work has any value. If the work survives, that builder will receive a reward. But if the work is burned up, the builder will suffer great loss. The builder will be saved [will get into heaven], but like someone barely escaping through a wall of flames" (NLT).

That's why I spend as much time as possible with people I call "first love" Christians. They're "family," we're going to spend eternity together, and we've determined to make the best use of our time to bring as many people as possible to Jesus while there's still time. It's too wonderful to comprehend! Out of the billions of people who have lived on this earth over millions of years, God chose us to represent Him in these last days for mankind. How could anything else in our lives be more important? No matter where you are in your spiritual journey, it's now insanely important to identify and spend time with those who will lift you up spiritually and, if you're not saved, get you saved.

It's time to ask yourself, Am I a believer?

SCRIPTURES FOR DEEPER REFLECTION

- **Beware of wolves in sheep's clothing:** Matthew 7:21–23 (NLT)

- **Not doing the first work (sharing your faith) causes you to lose your testimony:** Revelation 2:5 (NKJV)

- **When God is your first love, you'll openly declare Him:** Romans 10:9 (NLT)

- **It's possible to be an exalted church leader without being saved:** Matthew 7:22–23 (NLT)

- **God is our ultimate judge:** Romans 12:19 (KJV)

- **It's never been more important to be in church:** Hebrews 10:25 (NLT)

- **Most of us are working on a fraction of our potential:** John 14:12 (NLT)

- **You can't take credit for your entrance into heaven:** Ephesians 2:8 (NLT)

- **Faith without works is dead and useless:** James 2:14 (NLT)

- **Simply knowing Jesus is the Son of God does not get you into heaven:** James 2:19 (NLT)

- **You have to listen for God's voice amid the noise of this world:** 2 Corinthians 4:4 (NLT)

- **This is life's most important decision!** Joshua 24:15 (KJV)

- **Rampant apostasy confirms we're in the last days:** 1 Timothy 4:1 (NLT)

- **People are desperate; now is the time to let our light shine:** Matthew 5:16 (KJV)

- **These are the "times of the signs":** Luke 21:28 (NIV)

- **Reading the Word is useless unless you do what it says!** James 1:22 (NIV)

- **Don't let Satan and the cares of this world rob you of your joy:** Mark 4:19 (NKJV)

- **You don't want to barely make it into heaven:** 1 Corinthians 3:13–15 (NLT)

CHAPTER 23

INTIMACY WITH GOD

IWAS RECENTLY AT a luncheon for a nationally known politician running for high public office. During the Q&A, I asked him if he had a belief system that impacted how he lived his life. When he referenced God as "a higher power," it told me everything I needed to know about the man. When you have a personal relationship with Jesus Christ, you don't describe Him as a higher power.

The "Big Guy in the sky" is another term people often use when they want to sound spiritual but have no idea what they're talking about. What they're saying is, like 99 percent of the people who have ever lived on planet Earth, they believe there's a God out there somewhere. Romans 1:20 tells us: "Ever since the world was created, people have seen the earth and sky. Through everything God made, they can clearly see his invisible qualities—his eternal power and divine nature. So they have no excuse for not knowing God" (NLT).

We're only accountable for what we know. And what Romans 1 tells us is that even in the most primitive of cultures, man instinctively knows there's a higher power. But with added information comes a higher level of understanding and accountability. America has been the most Christian nation in the world, with near zero possibility for anyone in America not to have heard the gospel message innumerable times. How is it possible for anyone in America to only know God as a higher power today? I understand that politicians are often afraid to show their hand on subjects like religion and choose to be noncommittal. But those who have a personal relationship with Jesus Christ will immediately see those moments as opportunities to share their faith.

It's common knowledge that second-generation people are rarely as passionate and devoted to anything as their parents were. I'm an anomaly. I represent the third generation of a family business that multiplied greatly under my watch. But most family businesses fail to survive their second generation of ownership. There's a crossover to the church in this dynamic.

A generation of parents who replicated the faith of their parents presumed their kids would do the same. But they didn't. Proverbs 22:6 tells us: "Train up a child in the way he should go: and when he is old, he will not depart from it" (KJV). But two-thirds (66 percent) of kids who grew up in church are turning their backs on God by the time they graduate college.[1] The problem is, we didn't train them in the ways they should go when they were kids.

Parents presumed the church would train their kids, while our youth pastors have been entertaining our kids to draw crowds. With only 12 percent of our youth pastors having a biblical worldview,[2] the focus has been on music instead of worship, messages to entertain rather than convict, and mission trips without a mission. The end result has been graduating high schoolers completely unprepared for godless professors. We now have a generation of formerly "Christian kids" who are now "Christian adults" still believing themselves to be Christian but who are in reality biblically illiterate.

This is how we have 70 percent of our population identifying themselves as Christians, with only 22 percent of our population currently going to church on a regular basis—and political candidates referring to God as a higher power. How far we have fallen! More than half of our population holds in high esteem the term "being religious." I mentioned earlier that I'm often described as being religious, while I abhor the term. Religion is man's vain attempt to please God with a list of dos and don'ts. But if we do all of them and have not love, what good is it? All of this plays to a view of God as being a distant judge who judges us by our outward actions. But Ephesians 2:9 explains that our salvation is not of works, lest any man should boast.

BEWARE OF FALSE DOCTRINES

Navigating through life today with limited Bible knowledge, a ton of man's distorted views of God, and pulpits preaching false doctrines makes it a challenge to really know who God is and how

He relates to your life. Quite frankly, it's hard to find a church preaching sound doctrine today. When I'm in California, I drive forty-five minutes to get to Jack Hibbs at Calvary Chapel Chino Hills, and thirty minutes when I'm in Arizona to get to Dream City Church, where I can be fed every Sunday. Both are proclaiming the Word of God, and both are available online.

Thank God, we have the great pulpits of America available to us online on demand. It's incredible. But make no mistake; there's no substitution for coming together for corporate worship and praise and the proclamation of the Word. I've never enjoyed being in church as much as the first day Jack Hibbs reopened his doors during the pandemic, in spite of California's Governor Newsom. We literally ran into the sanctuary, sang from our bootstraps, and listened as Jack proclaimed the Word. After being forced to settle for online church services and then coming back into fellowship, you know immediately why Hebrews 10:25 tells us: "Let us not neglect our meeting together, as some people do, but encourage one another, especially now that the day of his return is drawing near" (NLT).

The contrast of where the world is today in their relationship with God, to where most Christians are today in their relationship with God, to where God wants us to be with Him every day is striking. This is the same God who speaks worlds into existence (Heb. 11:3), knows every thought you've ever had (Heb. 4:12), never leaves you or forsakes you (Heb. 13:5), wants to be your friend (John 15:15), thinks about you constantly (Ps. 139:17), has a perfect plan for your life (Jer. 29:11), and is ready to direct your steps (Prov. 3:5–6) to give you a life exceedingly abundantly above anything you could ask for or imagine (Eph. 3:20). God is anything but the world's view of a distant God sitting in judgment of your every move. He loves you!

In his book *A New Song* written in the 1970s, Pat Boone said it's like having a bank account full of money and never writing a check. He was speaking of the power of the Holy Spirit operating in our lives. Do you understand you have the resources of almighty God? It only takes the faith of a little child to trust the scriptures you already know to put them to use. You can start by believing all the scriptures just mentioned in the previous paragraph. They're all true!

IT'S IMPOSSIBLE TO BELIEVE THE SCRIPTURES WITHOUT GETTING EXCITED!

You see, it's impossible to believe these scriptures without getting excited and telling everyone. And when we realize He's always there, how foolish can we be not to talk with Him? It took me decades to figure this out. I couldn't comprehend 1 Thessalonians 5:16–18: "Rejoice always, pray without ceasing, give thanks in all circumstances; for this is the will of God in Christ Jesus for you" (ESV). I couldn't imagine ever doing that.

I struggled to pray once a day! And that was only out of obligation. It wasn't until I started sharing my faith that I began talking to God without ceasing. I needed direction on who to share my faith with and what to say. It happened so naturally and so easily that I didn't even realize it was happening. It was like having a new electronic gadget and not knowing how to operate it. I needed help, and there was no one else to go to.

I was determined to start sharing my faith. I knew I was in way over my head and found myself desperately asking God for His help. And then the opportunities to share my faith started increasing, and it just hit me one day that I was praying without ceasing. I couldn't believe it! This may be the main reason God wants us to share our faith—to have intimacy with Him.

Moving everyone you encounter, every day, closer to Jesus automatically leads you into a continual conversation with God. You can't help yourself. I know it must sound crazy, but I find myself actually strategizing with God, like we're partners. I'm literally talking to Him in my head and feeling His direction. I don't know any other way to experience this level of intimacy with God. All this time we've been avoiding sharing our faith, feeling it's not our job or that we're not qualified or whatever. Sadly, we've not been given good direction on why we should share our faith.

Had we been told it was the ultimate way to know and believe and understand that He is God and to have intimacy with Him, 100 percent of us would be sharing our faith, and we would be living in an entirely different world!

SCRIPTURES FOR DEEPER REFLECTION

- **No one has an excuse for not knowing there is a God:** Romans 1:20 (NLT)

- **We're paying the price for not getting our kids saved when they were kids:** Proverbs 22:6 (KJV)

- **Most Christians believe you can earn your way into heaven:** Ephesians 2:8–9 (NLT)

- **Church attendance is at an all-time low:** Hebrews 10:25 (NLT)

- **God spoke the universe into existence:** Hebrews 11:3 (KJV)

- **God knows your every thought and intention:** Hebrews 4:12 (ESV)

- **God never leaves you:** Hebrews 13:5 (NIV)

- **God is your friend:** John 15:15 (NLT)

- **God thinks about you constantly:** Psalm 139:17 (NLT)

- **God has plans for you:** Jeremiah 29:11 (NIV)

- **When you trust God wholeheartedly, He will direct your paths:** Proverbs 3:5–6 (KJV)

- **God loves to overachieve:** Ephesians 3:20 (NKJV)

- **You pray without ceasing when you move everyone, every day, closer to Jesus:** 1 Thessalonians 5:16–18 (ESV)

CHAPTER 24

GOD IS HOLDING YOU ACCOUNTABLE

THERE'S A SOBERING passage in Ezekiel 3 that should cause us all great concern. Of course, Ezekiel was an Old Testament prophet living under the law, so there's not a direct connection to what God told Ezekiel and what He is telling us today—and yet there is. God's nature and concern for the lost never changes.

In Ezekiel's time walled cities kept watchmen on their walls to warn them of impending danger. God used that fact to make His point to Ezekiel—and perhaps to us—that Ezekiel was a "watchman on the wall," and if he failed to warn the people that the enemy (Satan) was coming, they would die in their sins, but their blood would be on Ezekiel's hands. And God told that to one of His elect prophets! What about us? Now's the time to be thankful that we're living under the New Covenant, saved by grace and not of works.

God warned His faithful servant and prophet that He was holding him accountable for warning those around him that the enemy had determined to take them to hell. It's not a stretch to believe that God's expectations are the very same for us. There is no greater task set before us. As we near the end of this book, it's time to get serious with those of you who are on the end of the diving board and still afraid to take the plunge—unsure whether you want to make a total commitment to whatever God has planned for your life.

A mixture of enjoying who you are now and fearing you might become a different person is a powerful deterrent to halfhearted Christians. The question is, Do you want to remain halfhearted? Frankly, it's not a fun place to be. Matthew 6:24 explains it well: "No one can serve two masters. Either you will hate the one and love the other, or you will be devoted to the one and despise the other." James 1:6–7 provides the added dimension that being double-minded removes God's obligation to answer your prayers: "For he that wavereth is like a wave of the sea driven with the wind and tossed. For let not that man think that he shall receive any thing of the Lord" (KJV).

Just a quick reminder that it's impossible to have faith if you don't know God is answering your prayers. And without faith, everything about your walk with God falls apart. Without faith, it's impossible to please God. Without faith, you can't escape living your life in fear, like over 80 percent of all Americans, including Christians. It's tragic, but the statistics confirm that's exactly where most Christians are today.

IT'S TIME TO TAKE CHARGE

For the most part, American Christians have become people of faith who are living without faith and unable to share their faith. It's time to take charge of your personal relationship with God and come out from among those who are treading water and getting tired. If we're in the last days heading to the Antichrist, anything less than wholehearted faith is not going to serve you well.

**IT'S TIME TO
TAKE CHARGE**

Romans 5:1–2 gives us a glorious picture of who we are in Christ and how we should be living our lives: "Therefore, since we have been made right in God's sight by faith, we have peace with God because of what Jesus Christ our Lord has done for us. Because of our faith, Christ has brought us into this place of undeserved privilege where we now stand, and we confidently and joyfully look forward to sharing God's glory" (NLT).

This scripture is worth reading repeatedly because it summarizes, in one verse, what our lives here on earth should look like from the time of our salvation to our last breath. We've been made right in God's sight; we have peace, faith, and undeserved privilege; and we joyfully (not reluctantly) look forward to sharing our faith and God's glory.

This is the standard by which we all should be living our lives. This is what life looks like when you take the plunge into allowing God to wholly and completely become the Lord of your life. When you're all-in, you'll be shouting it from the housetops. And if you're not doing that, you're not there yet. The degree to which you share your faith is your best barometer for self-judging your own relationship with God.

I do have good news if you're still worrying about becoming someone you don't want to be. I actually run from overbearing Christians, if that's your concern. The biggest change for me is that I do everything better! I try to do everything in my life in a way that honors God and attracts people to Him. But I'm still the same guy. I don't recall ever offending anyone or putting anyone off or appearing to be a zealot because of my love and obedience to God.

It's so easy to paraphrase scripture and hang our hats on the scriptures that best fit our comfort level. Ephesians 2:8–9 in isolation tells us: "For by grace you have been saved through faith, and that...not of works, lest anyone should boast" (NKJV). That would seem to get you off the hook for doing anything more than accepting Jesus Christ as your Savior and Lord. But the very next verse (v. 10) shatters that thought by saying: "For we are His workmanship, created in Christ Jesus for good works, which God prepared beforehand that we should walk in them" (NKJV). While we're not saved by works, we are saved for good works, most importantly living for God's work, leading people to Him.

Everything else pales in comparison with leading one person to the Lord. Luke 15:10 echoes that viewpoint from heaven: "In the same way, I tell you, there is joy in the presence of the angels of God over one sinner who repents" (NASB). On a personal basis, the joy of knowing I had something to do with one person accepting Jesus Christ as their Savior and Lord blows away the biggest order I've ever generated for our car wax. Mind you, big orders get me excited—like "shouting" excited. But leading someone to the Lord is eternal. I'll be celebrating those events billions of years from now.

Think about that! It's mind-boggling and so dwarfs whatever problems and victories are capturing your emotions at this moment.

And it's always and forever a team sport, with every salvation being preceded by multiple team members doing their part. I just received word about a waitress in Bakersfield, California, who was nonplussed when I offered to pray for any need she might have. I was with a group that morning that included Jennifer, whose husband is the president of a ministry I love called CityServe. That one seed led to questions from the waitress that eventually led to her salvation, and now she's leading people to the Lord. All because I asked her if there was anything I could pray for her about over a year ago. Most of the time we won't know the fruit we bear until we get to heaven.

There's a famous football story I love about "winning one for the Gipper." Knute Rockne was the football coach for Notre Dame back in the 1920s. He was having a bad year and was losing a big game. At halftime, he used the words of his former halfback, George Gip, to inspire his team. When George Gip was dying in the hospital, George asked Knute to tell his team, at some point when they really needed an extra boost, to "win one for the Gipper." So Coach Rockne told that story like no one else could, and the underdog Irish went on to win that game 12-6.[1]

I know this is a stretch, but this is who I am. When I'm working hard at leading a challenging unbeliever to the Lord, I often hear Jesus saying, "Win this one for Me. I died for them!"

SCRIPTURES FOR DEEPER REFLECTION

- **God is holding us accountable:** Ezekiel 3:17–18 (KJV)

- **This is not the time to be half-hearted with God:** Matthew 6:24 (KJV)

- **Being half-hearted ends God's obligation to answer your prayers:** James 1:6–8 (KJV)

- **Living in God's "undeserved privilege" compels you to share His glory:** Romans 5:1–2 (NLT)

- **We're saved by grace and created for good works:** Ephesians 2:8–10 (NKJV)

- **There's no greater high than the high that comes from leading someone to Jesus:** Luke 15:10 (NKJV)

CHAPTER 25

YOU'RE RUNNING OUT OF TIME!

THROUGHOUT THE ENTIRETY of this book, I allude to the fact that time may be short between now and when we see the Lord face-to-face. Whether that's true or not has no bearing on the message of this book. But it seems prudent to explain this thought more clearly for those who have no knowledge of God's time clock. I doubt that the Lord will return today, but He could. And if He did, what would that mean for you and your family and your friends?

No matter where you are in your relationship with God, you're running out of time! If you haven't accepted Jesus Christ as your Savior and Lord yet, you're literally playing with fire and running out of time. If you never share your faith and have unsaved friends and loved ones, you're running out of time to reach them. And if you're already sharing your faith, you need to up your game! All of us are running out of time!

The timing of this book is not by accident. Prior to right now, it would have largely fallen on deaf ears. God knew that and supernaturally orchestrated the events required to bring this book out right when it's becoming obvious that these are the last days.

I realize that's an offense to those of you who love this world, and it all but destroys my credibility. That's why I'll let the Bible speak for itself. I'm only reporting on what the Scriptures are telling us. Over two thousand years ago, God explained in detail what we're seeing today!

It's important you understand how we operate in a sea of choices and opportunities. In street terms, it really boils down to whether you're feeding your flesh or your spirit. When your focus is on fleshly desires, the things of this world will capture your mind and direct your actions. Things like honoring God and being led by the Spirit will have no attraction.

But when you feed your Spirit with spiritual thoughts, your mind follows that path and an entirely new world of freedom and joy and excitement will flood your soul and set you free. I'm a car guy with an insatiable love for beautiful cars with great design and perfect paint finishes. They're my life in this world, and I enjoy them to their fullest. But they're not my "treasure."

My treasure has nothing to do with this world. Matthew 6:19–20 says it perfectly: "Do not lay up for yourselves treasures on earth, where moth and rust destroy and where thieves break in and steal; but lay up for yourselves treasures in heaven, where neither moth nor rust destroys and where thieves do not break in and steal. For where your treasure is, there your heart will be also" (NKJV). What owns your heart?

It's an amazing time to be alive. So many people are sensing the uncertainty of our days while staying committed to not accepting their spiritual significance—trying to believe that things will return to normal with increasing uncertainty. Over 80 percent of the unchurched would like to believe there's a God who can make sense out of the chaos and are looking for someone to tell them. That's why it's never been easier to lead people to Jesus.

But, as if they're hedging their bet, many are spending money like they know for sure things are going to get better. A record $469 million worth of collector cars was sold in five days at auctions in Monterey, California, during the week of the 2022 Pebble Beach Concours d'Elegance. The average sales price per car was $590,700.[1]

I admit, I'm a car guy, and I was enjoying the action. The cars were as breathtaking as the prices and worth every penny. But every one of them was purchased with the belief that life as we know it is going to continue—in the face of overwhelming evidence to the contrary. People desperately want to believe that life is going to return to normal.

As I sat in one of the auctions enjoying the theater of the moment with great euphoria, the passage in Matthew 24:37 came to me: "The Arrival of the Son of Man will take place in times like Noah's. Before the great flood everyone was carrying on as usual, having a good time right up to the day Noah boarded the ark. They knew nothing—until the flood hit and swept everything away" (MSG).

When you sow seeds to your spirit, your interest in the things of this world changes. It's not that you can't enjoy the things of this world. You just hold them loosely in your hands and use them for God's glory until the "trumpet of God" sounds. (See 1 Thessalonians 4:16, NKJV.) When that happens, you'll see Him face-to-face and never look back.

As long as God remains your first love, you can't be disappointed. It's impossible! When anything else becomes your god, it will involve man and you'll always be disappointed. "The human heart is the most deceitful of all things, and desperately wicked. Who really knows how bad it is?" (Jer. 17:9, NLT). The only thing in the entire universe that never moves and can be fully trusted is God.

First John 2:15–17 (NLT) says it perfectly:

> Do not love this world nor the things it offers you, for when you love the world, you do not have the love of the Father in you. For the world offers only a craving for physical pleasure, a craving for everything we see, and pride in our achievements and possessions. These are not from the Father but are from this world. And this world is fading away, along with every-thing that people crave. But anyone who does what pleases God will live forever.

Again, for those who are looking up with expectation, the rapture of the church could happen at any moment. First Thessalonians 4:16–17 describes how Christians will soon be removed from this world: "For the Lord himself shall descend from heaven with a shout, with the voice of the archangel, and with the trump of God: and the dead in Christ shall rise first: Then we which are alive and remain shall be caught up together with them in the clouds, to meet the Lord in the air: and so shall we ever be with the Lord" (KJV).

First Corinthians 15:52 adds: "It will happen in a moment, in the blink of an eye, when the last trumpet is blown. For when the trumpet sounds, those who have died will be raised to live forever. And we who are living will also be transformed" (NLT).

So many Christians cringe when I mention that the rapture can happen at any minute. But you only do that when you don't want to let go of this world. I'm more than ready, and I'd rather avoid the chaos that's on our doorstep. But I also need more time to get the people I'm praying for into heaven.

REMOVING ALL DOUBT

If you have any doubt about these being the last days, 2 Timothy 3:1–5

REMOVING ALL DOUBT

removes all doubt: "There will be terrible times in the last days. People will be lovers of themselves, lovers of money, boastful, proud, abusive, disobedient to their parents, ungrateful, unholy, without love, unforgiving, slanderous, without self-control, brutal, not lovers of the good, treacherous, rash, conceited, lovers of pleasure rather than lovers of God—having a form of godliness but denying its power." This is the world we're living in, described to us by the apostle Paul over two thousand years ago.

Matthew 24:37 likens what we see today to the days of Noah: "As it was in the days of Noah, so it will be at the coming of the Son of Man." Genesis 6:5 tells us what it was like in the days of Noah that mirrors what we're seeing today, and it's dead-on: "The LORD saw how great the wickedness of the human race had become on the earth, and that every inclination of the thoughts of the human heart was only evil all the time."

I don't know about you, but I wonder how these people who don't know God ever sleep at night with so much evil coming at us "all the time." I get my news feed right after I wake up in the morning, and the world is already at it, doing its thing. The grand orchestration of what we're seeing is clearly supernatural, and it's breathtaking!

Along with His warnings, God gives us directions on how to live our lives in the last days. Ephesians 5:15–17 explains: "So be careful how you live. Don't live like fools, but like those who are wise. Make the most of every opportunity in these evil days. Don't act thoughtlessly, but understand what the Lord wants you to do" (NLT). Ephesians 6:13 goes on to say: "Therefore, put on every piece of God's armor so you will be able to resist the enemy in the time of evil. Then after the battle you will still be standing firm" (NLT).

Bible prophecy provides the greatest proof that God is real and the Scriptures are authentic. How else could the prophets explain a thousand years in advance the birth, life, death, and resurrection of Jesus Christ without one error? And how could they so perfectly describe the signs of the times that we're now seeing with our very own eyes?

And now I'll tell you my reason for writing this book. Of course, I'm anxious for you to discover how easy it is to *Ignite Your Life* and have the time of your life for the rest of your life. It's the timing that's critical. I'm convinced that time is short, the signs of the times are real, and millions of good people who believe in Jesus but have never accepted Him as their Savior are waking up. The last great awakening, inspired by a sovereign move of the Holy Spirit, is often referred to as the latter rain, the last great revival before the Lord returns. There are as many interpretations of this as there are theologians, which I am not. But it's hard for me to believe that the rapture will happen without God giving good people one more opportunity to come to Him.

And with that mindset, I love James 5:7–8, which tells us: "Be patient, therefore, brothers, until the coming of the Lord. See how the farmer waits for the precious fruit [new believers] of the earth, being patient about it, until it receives the early and the late rains. You also, be patient. Establish your hearts, for the coming of the Lord is at hand" (ESV).

Hell is a very real place reserved for Satan and his demons. In the words of Penn Jillette, "How much do you have to hate somebody to believe that everlasting life is possible and not tell them that?" Do you want to face almighty God knowing you didn't warn them? And do you want to miss out on being part of what may be the last and greatest revival of all time?

You're running out of time!

SCRIPTURES FOR DEEPER REFLECTION

- **Who or what owns your heart?**
  Matthew 6:19–20 (NKJV)

- **Are you focused on God's time clock or yours?**
  Matthew 24:37 (MSG)

- **Meanwhile, Satan and our own hearts are trying to deceive us:** Jeremiah 17:9 (NLT)

- **Anything you love more than God separates you from God:** 1 John 2:15–17 (NLT)

- **We're about to see Jesus face-to-face forever:**
  1 Thessalonians 4:16–17 (KJV)

- **It will happen in the "blink of an eye":**
  1 Corinthians 15:52 (NLT)

- **Bible prophecy describes the days we are in:**
  2 Timothy 3:1–4 (NIV)

- **As it was in the days of Noah:** Genesis 6:5 (NLT)

- **God wants to use you these days for His glory:**
  Ephesians 5:15–17 (NLT)

- **When you're in the battle, nothing can happen to you unless God allows it:** Ephesians 6:13 (NLT)

- **It's always God's timing, not yours!**
  James 5:7–8 (ESV)

CHAPTER 26

YOU HAVE THREE CHOICES

THEY SAY INFORMATION is power. Now that you've read this book, you have all the information—and the power—you need to make one of three choices that will determine how and where you spend eternity.

Before we go there, let's address what eternity is from the perspective of our finite minds. As hard as we try, eternity is actually beyond our comprehension. God lives outside of time, and so will we after we breathe our last breath. Eternity never ends! Just imagine: millions of millions of years from now, your eternity in heaven or hell will still be just beginning.

Our human frame of reference is finite. No matter how bad things get for us in this life, there's always an end to it. One of our most used phrases is "this too shall pass." A broken bone eventually heals. Even when disease leads to death, there's an end to the suffering. But eternity has no ending. The thought of going to hell with all its torment is terrifying to me. But there are no words to describe what it will be like in hell, knowing its horrors will never end.

You can't escape the fact that you're going to die; in fact, it could happen today. You could be in the middle of the next mass shooting. But many people refuse to think about eternity. I have so many friends my age who still refuse to think about it. They're too busy and too impor-

YOU CAN'T ESCAPE

tant, acting like they're going to live forever. Some are delaying the decision to serve God, and if they keep putting it off until they never make that choice, they will end up in hell. It's demonic deception! As long as Satan keeps you focused on this world rather than the next, he wins.

While all of us will make one of these three choices, some by default, the term *door* is more appropriate because whichever choice you make will be the door you walk through into eternity.

DOOR NUMBER 1: BELIEVING HELL DOESN'T EXIST

To deny the existence of hell is to repudiate the Bible, the existence of God, and everything that has been written in this book. It's entirely your right to do that if you so choose. But I would be remiss if I didn't share what the Bible says you'll experience if you reject God. To put it plainly: you'll be betting your eternity on the belief that the Bible is false and hell doesn't exist.

In itself, the repudiation of the Bible is a massive task. The chances of over forty different authors writing one cohesive book without divine inspiration over the span of about fifteen hundred years is zero. You can't get two authors living at the same time, writing on the same subject, to agree on everything. The odds of Jesus Christ fulfilling the more than three hundred prophecies documented in Scripture are incalculable. Many of the prophecies, such as where He was born, were beyond His control. And yet as we saw in the early part of this book, the prophecies describe what we're experiencing right now with the same specificity.

Add to that the fact that original manuscripts from great thinkers such as Aristotle number in the single digits. There are well over fourteen thousand original manuscripts confirming the authenticity of Scripture.[1] And the Bible blows the socks off all the *New York Times* best sellers every year, having sold billions of copies in more than seven hundred languages worldwide.[2] The Bible is by far the top-selling book of all time. It's seriously hard to believe the Bible is not God's inspired Word.

Having said that, let's look at what the Bible has to say about hell.

- Your name is entered into the Lamb's Book of Life when you're saved. But "anyone whose name was not found written in the Book of Life was cast into the lake of fire" (Rev. 20:15, MEV).

- Eternal life is God's gift, but we earn hell: "For the wages of sin is death [hell], but the gift of God is eternal life through Jesus Christ our Lord" (Rom. 6:23, MEV).

- Heaven and hell are eternal: "And they will go away into eternal punishment, but the righteous into eternal life" (Matt. 25:46, MEV).

- The fear (awe) of the Lord is the beginning of wisdom: "Do not fear those who kill the body but are not able to kill the soul. But rather fear Him who is able to destroy both soul and body in hell" (Matt. 10:28, MEV).

- Those who don't accept salvation will be banished forever from the presence of the Lord: "They shall be punished with eternal destruction, isolated from the presence of the Lord and from the glory of His power" (2 Thess. 1:9, MEV).

- There will be endless weeping in hell: "...and throw them into the blazing furnace, where there will be weeping and gnashing of teeth" (Matt. 13:50).

- Hell was prepared for Satan and his demons: "Then he will say to those on his left, 'Depart from me, you who are cursed, into the eternal fire prepared for the devil and his angels'" (Matt. 25:41).

- It's appointed unto man once to die and then the
  judgment: "But the cowardly, the unbelieving, the
  abominable, the murderers, the sexually immoral, the
  sorcerers, the idolaters, and all liars shall have their
  portion in the lake which burns with fire and brim-
  stone. This is the second death" (Rev. 21:8, MEV).

- The torment in hell never ends. It is where "their
  worm does not die and the fire is not quenched"
  (Mark 9:46, NKJV).

- The fire of hell is mixed with sulfur: "They will be
  tormented with burning sulfur in the presence of the
  holy angels and of the Lamb" (Rev. 14:10).

- God's breath sets hell afire: "The breath of the LORD,
  like a stream of burning sulfur, sets it ablaze" (Isa.
  30:33).

- It's not our lifeless bodies that are thrown into the
  fire: "The two of them were thrown alive into the
  fiery lake of burning sulfur" (Rev. 19:20).

- No one cares who you are in hell—you're alone
  in total darkness forever: "Fire resides in his tent;
  burning sulfur is scattered over his dwelling. His
  roots dry up below and his branches wither above.
  The memory of him perishes from the earth; he has
  no name in the land. He is driven from light into the
  realm of darkness and is banished from the world"
  (Job 18:15–18).

Now consider what people have said about hell over the years.

- Dante Alighieri: "The darkest places in hell are reserved for those who maintain their neutrality in times of moral crisis."[3]

- David Wilkerson: "The end of all we know is near—and we are busy playing with our toys!"[4]

- Randy Alcorn: "He who thinks he's not drowning won't reach for the life preserver."[5]

- Billy Graham: "If we had more hell in the pulpit, we would have less hell in the pew."[6]

- Leonard Ravenhill: "Better for you to have one sleepless night on earth than millions in hell."[7]

- Charles Spurgeon: "Still the soul seeth written o'er its head, 'Thou art damned for ever.' It heareth howlings that are to be perpetual; it seeth flames which are unquenchable; it knoweth pains that are unmitigated."[8]

- Billy Sunday: "Hell is the highest reward that the devil can offer you for being a servant of his."[9]

- John MacArthur: "People do not have to do something to go to hell; they just have to do nothing."[10]

- Charles Spurgeon: "Oh, my brothers and sisters in Christ, if sinners will be damned, at least let them leap to hell over our bodies; and if they will perish, let them perish with our arms about their knees, imploring them to stay, and not madly to destroy themselves. If hell must be filled, at least let it be filled in the teeth of our exertions and let not one go there unwarned and un-prayed for."[11]

These are just of few of the more than one hundred scriptures, written over a span of fifteen hundred years, and a short list of famous quotes that describe the realities of hell.

I can't overstate the horrors that await those who refuse to accept Jesus Christ as their Lord and Savior. And it needs to be abundantly clear: if you wait too long to make your choice and die before you decide to follow Jesus, you will spend eternity in hell. This is not the time to sugarcoat this message. You're literally playing with fire every day you delay your decision to follow Jesus. May I suggest that you go to SeekingGod.org right now to get that issue settled?

It's terrifying that the fear of hell, which is half the gospel, is almost nonexistent today because hell has rarely been preached from church pulpits for a generation. God went out of His way to present to us the ultimate reward and punishment options to give us the ultimate motivation to make the right choice: to accept Jesus Christ as our Lord. But we removed that motivation by no longer talking about hell, and as a result we have lost almost all fear of hell.

When faced with the choice between heaven and hell, both of which are clearly described in the Bible, it's what you call a no-brainer. I mean, who wants to spend forever in total darkness and complete isolation with fire and sulfur and demons, knowing the torment is never going to end?

May I suggest this is not the door you want to walk through?

DOOR NUMBER 2: SITTING ON THE BENCH

I don't need to spend as much time explaining this option because those of you who have made this choice already know it. With a long list of your own personal excuses, you're part of that over 80 percent of all Americans, including Christians, who live in fear and are upset over most of what you are seeing in the world today and feel powerless to stop it.

Preaching about the seriousness of lukewarmness is just as absent from our pulpits today as the subject of hell. Quite frankly, pastors have moved away from serious subjects for fear of offending and losing their congregations. Most church attenders today, wanting their ears tickled, are no longer tolerant of convicting, life-changing sermons. Pastors now serve mini-sermons to mini-Christians in time-sensitive rather than Holy Spirit-sensitive services.

In my travels around the country, I've found that typical faithful church attenders are discouraged, worried about everything, and know there's something missing in their lives. They long for the old days when God was moving and doing great things. (Of course, He still is moving and even more so today.) In short, they want to have their lives ignited. And after every one of those brief conversations, I wish they could see how little they would have to do to ignite themselves. So I decided to write this book for those tired of being tired.

Every chapter of this book was written with this group in mind. I don't need to repeat what I've already shared in these pages, but this is my opportunity to explain the seriousness of doing nothing. Just as there are continuing themes throughout the Bible on important subjects such as sharing your faith, there are also themes about doing nothing with your faith.

To repeat the stats one more time, over 80 percent of unchurched people already have at least one Christian in their lives that they trust. We could ignite America with revival in thirty days if we each took personal responsibility for our own worlds. You can't change the whole world, but you can change *your* world. And if all thirty million of us changed *our* worlds, we'd change the world.

But of far greater importance is what sharing your faith will do for you. This book is packed with scriptures telling you how sharing your faith will ignite your life.

It's your choice, and I want to help you make that decision. It's more than frightening to read the scriptures that target Christians who are sitting on the bench and doing nothing. I don't know about you, but I don't want to get spewed out of God's mouth. Revelation 3:15–17 is specifically written for Christians who are neither cold (ignoring God) nor hot (living for God's purpose, which is to seek and save the lost).

Here again is what Revelation 3:15–17 says:

I know your deeds, that you are neither cold nor hot. I wish you were either one or the other! So, because you are luke-warm—neither hot nor cold—I am about to spit you out of my mouth. You say, "I am rich; I have acquired wealth and do not need a thing." But you do not realize that you are wretched, pitiful, poor, blind and naked.

I know it's counterintuitive, but God often uses cold people to *move* non-Christians closer to Jesus. And Christians who are hot *move* people closer to Jesus for obvious reasons. But lukewarm Christians move people away from Jesus, with lower standards of conduct and turning people against God. Some of us are witnesses for the prosecution!

I love John 15:11, which tells us that when we bear fruit (lead others to Christ), God's joy will remain with us, and our joy will remain full. I know the truth of that scripture because I experienced it before I read it. I'm in perpetual joy because I'm always coming off one fruitful conversation and heading for another one.

But if you back up a few verses, you see an entirely different fate for the branches that don't bear fruit:

Yes, I am the vine; you are the branches. Those who remain in me, and I in them, will produce much fruit. For apart from me you can do nothing. Anyone who does not remain in me is thrown away like a useless branch and withers. Such branches are *gathered into a pile to be burned*.
—JOHN 15:5–6, NLT, EMPHASIS ADDED

I would say these scriptures are adequate motivators for getting anyone off the bench and into the game—and that hell is a moti-vator for choosing Jesus! It's too late in the game to just sit on the bench and complain about everything. And the longer you sit there, the longer you want to sit there. It's called spiritual atrophy, and it's deadly.

Here's one more passage of Scripture that you likely know well. The parable of the talents, in Matthew 25:14–30, says it all. It's a repetition of the same theme. For the one who did nothing with what he was given—never shared the good news he had received—even what he had was taken from him. Have you noticed how quickly you'll forget a great sermon or Scripture verse if you don't repeat it? If you don't use it, you lose it.

But then it gets far more serious. The end directive for the one who did nothing (sat on the bench) is terrifying. Look at what Matthew 25:30 says: "And cast the worthless servant into the outer darkness. In that place there will be weeping and gnashing of teeth" (ESV). None of us wants to go where there is darkness and gnashing of teeth!

I'm hoping I just blew you out of your comfort zone. God's patience eventually runs out for those of us He's given the good news to who are doing nothing with it. Compare that with knowing that God wants to direct your steps, explode your faith, fill your life with joy, and make everything in your life work for good.

I think the next door is a better choice for you!

DOOR NUMBER 3: IGNITING YOUR LIFE!

Imagine waking up every morning knowing (1) everything that happens that day is going to work for good, even the bad stuff that would normally rob you of your joy; (2) while many things may make you happy and unhappy that day, your joy in the Lord will never waver because you're always living for His purpose and bearing the fruit of new believers; and (3) God has already set your divine appointments for that day, will nudge you into every one of them, and will give you the words to say when you need them—as you walk confidently in the fellowship and friendship of God. No matter where you are or what you're facing, this is the life God wants you to have! This is life's great reward!

The number-one thing you don't want to do is what opens the door to having the time of your life for the rest of your life. Who doesn't want to live a life free of worry and full of joy, knowing God is making everything in your life work for good? Who doesn't want to be part of a team that's moving everyone, every day, closer to Jesus? And who doesn't want to have the intimacy with God that only comes through knowing He's using you to bring people to Him? At the very least, would you please try?

My friend Tony was out on his morning run and ran past an elderly Asian man who could barely walk. But God told him to go back to that Asian man and share his faith. Tony had every reason not to go back, including the potential language barrier. But he kept hearing God say, "Try! Try!" So Tony obediently turned around and ran back to walk with this elderly Asian man, who, as it turned out, spoke English. To Tony's surprise, the conversation quickly led to God and eternal life. At that point, Tony asked the man for his name. And the man said, "My name is Try." The man's name was Try! You can't make this stuff up!

If your life experiences have conditioned you to believe it's not worth "trying" to lead those around you to the Lord, you have no idea what you're missing! God is allowing our days to grow increasingly evil and supernatural to capture the hearts of millions of people He still wants to usher into heaven before the rapture. Even the hardest of hearts are recognizing their need for God today. We're on the cusp of what may be the greatest revival of all time as God sovereignly moves on the hearts of the lost *and* the saved as he ignites Christians to ignite America with revival, one person at a time.

With nearly 80 percent of our population rarely if ever going to church, you may be the only hope people will have to learn that God loves them and wants them to spend eternity with Him. I pray that you can grasp the excitement and importance of what this statement means for them and for you!

God's insistence that you share your faith is driven by His knowledge of what sharing your faith does for *you*—and what happens if you don't. We covered the "don't" in chapter 11 on spiritual atrophy. The truth of this book is solid as a rock because it's all Scripture, with none being more important than this one: "'You are My witnesses,' says the LORD, 'and My servant whom I have chosen, that you may know and believe Me, and understand that I am He.

Before Me there was no God formed, nor shall there be after Me'" (Isa. 43:10, NKJV).

God knows that when you live for His purpose to seek and save the lost—to move everyone, every day, closer to Jesus—there's no question that you will know and believe and understand that He is God! It's time for you to experience this truth for yourself by getting off the bench and into your rewards—both here and for eternity.

See you there!

Barry

SCRIPTURES FOR DEEPER REFLECTION

- **Your name is entered into the Lamb's Book of Life when you're saved:** Revelation 20:15 (MEV)

- **Eternal life is God's gift, but we earn hell:** Romans 6:23 (MEV)

- **Heaven and hell are eternal:** Matthew 25:46 (MEV)

- **The fear (awe) of the Lord is the beginning of wisdom:** Matthew 10:28 (MEV)

- **Those who don't accept salvation will be banished forever from the presence of the Lord:** 2 Thessalonians 1:9 (MEV); Matthew 13:50 (NIV); Matthew 25:41 (NIV)

- **It's appointed unto man once to die and then the judgment:** Revelation 21:8 (MEV)

- **The torment in hell never ends:** Mark 9:46 (NKJV); Revelation 14:10 (NIV)

- **God would prefer that you be either cold or hot!** Revelation 3:15–17 (NIV)

- **When we bear fruit, God's joy remains with us:** John 15:11 (ESV)

- **There are consequences for those who don't bear fruit:** John 15:5–6 (NLT); Matthew 25:14–30 (ESV)

- **The "lostness" of your unsaved friends is all the motivation you need:** Isaiah 43:10 (NKJV)

NOTES

CHAPTER 4

1. Benjamin Clary, "Mood of the Nation: Majority of Americans Are 'Extremely Worried' About the Country in 2022," APM Research Lab, January 12, 2022, https://www.apmresearchlab.org/motn/hope-worry-2022.

CHAPTER 5

1. Jeffrey M. Jones, "Belief in God in U.S. Dips to 81%, a New Low," Gallup, June 17, 2022, https://news.gallup.com/poll/393737/belief-god-dips-new-low.aspx; Julia Mueller, "Record Percentage Says US Headed in Wrong Direction: NBC Poll," *The Hill*, August 21, 2022, https://thehill.com/homenews/administration/3609791-record-percentage-says-us-headed-in-wrong-direction-nbc-poll; "National: More Americans Struggling; Inflation, Gas Prices Top Family Concerns," Monmouth University Poll, July 5, 2022, https://www.monmouth.edu/polling-institute/documents/monmouthpoll_us_070522.pdf; "Satisfaction With the United States," Gallup 2022, accessed September 15, 2022, https://news.gallup.com/poll/1669/general-mood-country.aspx.

2. Aaron Earls, "Most Open to Spiritual Conversations, Few Christians Speaking," Lifeway Research, February 22, 2022, https://research.lifeway.com/2022/02/22/most-open-to-spiritual-conversations-few-christians-speaking.

3. Aaron Earls, "Christians Don't Share Faith With Unchurched Friends," Lifeway Research, September 9, 2021, https://research.lifeway.com/2021/09/09/christians-dont-share-faith-with-unchurched-friends.

4. Ian M. Giatti, "'Shocking' Survey Finds Only Half of Evangelical Pastors Hold Biblical Worldview," The Christian Post, May 29, 2022, https://www.christianpost.com/news/survey-only-half-of-evangelical-pastors-hold-biblical-worldview.html; "New George Barna Research: 'Dangerously' Low Percentage of Americans Have a Biblical Worldview," American Pastors Network, March 30,

2020, https://americanpastorsnetwork.net/2020/03/30/new-george-barna-research-dangerously-low-percentage-of-americans-have-a-biblical-worldview; Michael Gryboski, "Only 6% of Americans Have a 'Biblical Worldview,' Research From George Barna Finds," The Christian Post, May 26, 2021, https://www.christianpost.com/news/only-6-of-americans-have-a-biblical-worldview-survey.html.

CHAPTER 7

1. Beinzee, "A Gift of a Bible," YouTube, July 8, 2010, https://www.youtube.com/watch?v=6md638smQd8.

CHAPTER 10

1. Eric Liddell, "God Made Me Fast...," Brainy Quote, accessed August 8, 2022, https://www.brainyquote.com/quotes/eric_liddell_338714.

CHAPTER 11

1. "Barna: State of the Church," Barna, February 19, 2020, https://www.barna.com/research/current-perceptions.

2. Richard R. Beeman, PhD, "Perspectives on the Constitution: A Republic, If You Can Keep It," National Constitution Center, constitutioncenter.org, accessed July 25, 2022, https://constitutioncenter.org/learn/educational-resources/historical-documents/perspectives-on-the-constitution-a-republic-if-you-can-keep-it.

3. "From John Adams to Massachusetts Militia, 11 October 1798," Founders Online, founders.archives.gov, October 11, 1798, https://founders.archives.gov/documents/Adams/99-02-02-3102.

CHAPTER 13

1. "Americans: My Faith Isn't the Only Way to Heaven," Fox News, January 13, 2015, https://www.foxnews.com/story/americans-my-faith-isnt-the-only-way-to-heaven; "Americans Are Redefining the Faith: Adherents Creating New Worldviews

Loosely Tied to Biblical Teaching," Cultural Research Center, accessed September 15, 2022, https://www.arizonachristian.edu/wp-content/uploads/2020/10/CRC_AWVI2020_Release11_Digital_04_20201006.pdf.

2. "The Digital Pulpit: A Nationwide Analysis of Online Sermons," Pew Research Center, December 16, 2019, https://www.pewresearch.org/religion/2019/12/16/the-digital-pulpit-a-nationwide-analysis-of-online-sermons.

3. Aaron Earls, "Half of Churchgoers Have Never Heard of the Great Commission," Lifeway Research, March 28, 2018, https://research.lifeway.com/2018/03/28/half-of-churchgoers-have-never-heard-of-the-great-commission.

4. Aaron Earls, "20 Vital Stats for Ministry in 2020," Lifeway Research, January 7, 2020, https://research.lifeway.com/2020/01/07/20-vital-stats-for-ministry-in-2020.

5. "How Often Do You Attend Church or Synagogue—at Least Once a Week, Almost Every Week, About Once a Month, Seldom, or Never?," Statista, June 21, 2022, https://www.statista.com/statistics/245491/church-attendance-of-americans.

CHAPTER 14

1. Giatti, "'Shocking' Survey Finds Only Half of Evangelical Pastors Hold Biblical Worldview."

2. "New George Barna Research: 'Dangerously' Low Percentage of Americans Have a Biblical Worldview," American Pastors Network.

CHAPTER 16

1. Clary, "Mood of the Nation: Majority of Americans Are 'Extremely Worried' About the Country in 2022."

CHAPTER 21

1. Dr. Charles Stanley, "Satan's Strategy—In Touch," One Place, September 21, 2021, https://www.oneplace.com/devotionals/

in-touch-with-charles-stanley/satans-strategy-in-touch-
september-21-11638547.html.

CHAPTER 22

1. "The American Religious Landscape in 2020," PRRI, July 8, 2021,
   https://www.prri.org/research/2020-census-of-american-religion.

2. "How Often Do You Attend Church or Synagogue—at Least Once
   a Week, Almost Every Week, About Once a Month, Seldom, or
   Never?," Statista.

CHAPTER 23

1. Aaron Earl, "Did You Stop Attending Church Regularly (Twice a
   Month or More) for at Least a Year Between the Ages of 18 and
   22?," Lifeway Research, January 15, 2019, https://research.lifeway.
   com/2019/01/15/most-teenagers-drop-out-of-church-as-young-
   adults.

2. Dr. George Barna, "Release #5: Shocking Results Concerning
   the Worldview of Christian Pastors," Cultural Research Center,
   May 10, 2022, https://www.arizonachristian.edu/wp-content/
   uploads/2022/05/AWVI2022_Release05_Digital.pdf.

CHAPTER 24

1. Knute Rockne, "Win Just One for the Gipper," Schmoop, accessed
   August 1, 2022, https://www.shmoop.com/quotes/win-one-for-the-
   gipper.html.

CHAPTER 25

1. Robert Frank, "Classic Car Auctions in Monterey Score a Record
   $469 Million," CNBC, August 22, 2022, https://www.cnbc.
   com/2022/08/22/classic-car-auctions-in-monterey-score-a-record-
   456-million.html.

CHAPTER 26

1. Hank Hanegraaff, "Bible Reliability: M-A-P-S to Guide You Through Bible Reliability," Christian Research Institute, accessed August 9, 2022, https://www.equip.org/article/bible-reliability-m-a-p-s-to-guide-you-through-bible-reliability/.

2. "Our Impact," Wycliffe Bible Translators, accessed June 28, 2022, https://www.wycliffe.org.uk/about/our-impact/.

3. Dante Alighieri, "The Darkest Places in Hell...," Brainy Quote, accessed August 9, 2022, https://www.brainyquote.com/quotes/dante_alighieri_109737#:~:text=Dante%20Alighieri%20Quotes&text=The%20darkest%20places%20in%20hell%20are%20reserved%20for%20those%20who,in%20times%20of%20moral%20crisis.

4. David Wilkerson, "Love Not the World," World Challenge, March 19, 2015, https://www.worldchallenge.org/love-not-world.

5. Randy Alcorn, *The Grace and Truth Paradox* (New York: Crown Publishing, 2009), 75.

6. Billy Graham, "If We Had More Hell in the Pulpit...," AZ Quotes, accessed August 9, 2022, https://www.azquotes.com/quote/697878.

7. Leonard Ravenhill, "Better for You to Have One Sleepless Night...," AZ Quotes, accessed August 9, 2022, https://www.azquotes.com/quote/718802.

8. C. H. Spurgeon, "Free-Will—A Slave," sermon, New Park Street Chapel, December 2, 1855, Reformation Ireland, http://www.reformationireland.com/articles/free-will---a-slave/.

9. Billy Sunday Quotes, "Hell Is the Highest Reward...," QuoteFancy, accessed August 9, 2022, https://quotefancy.com/quote/1045062/Billy-Sunday-Hell-is-the-highest-reward-that-the-devil-can-offer-you-for-being-a-servant.

10. John F. MacArthur, "People Do Not Have to Do Something to Go to Hell...," All Christian Quotes, accessed August

9, 2022, https://www.allchristianquotes.org/quotes/John_F_
MacArthur/2102/.

11. Charles Haddon Spurgeon, *Sermons of the Rev. C. H. Spurgeon
    of London* (New York: Sheldon, Blakeman & Co., 1864), 333.

ABOUT THE AUTHOR

BARRY MEGUIAR IS the third-generation president of Meguiar's Car Wax. He grew the company from a small family business buffing cars in body shops to becoming the top-selling retail car wax in America and in countries around the world. His *Car Crazy* television show ran for eighteen years and aired globally on the Discovery Network. He has been honored with most of the major awards in the car hobby and is a SEMA Hall of Fame member. SEMA—the Specialty Equipment Market Association—is the largest automotive trade organization in the world.

Barry is a recipient of the National Religious Broadcasters' Billy Graham Award and Moody Bible's 1886 Legacy Award. He was honored with the Layman of the Year Award by Point Loma Nazarene University as well as the General Council of the Assemblies of God, where he served on the World Missions and Seminary Boards and led the Assemblies' Lay Ministries for two years. He also has an honorary doctorate from Northwest University.

As the founder/president of Ignite America, IgniteAmerica.com, and SeekingGod.com, Barry speaks nationally on the subject of igniting America with revival, one person at a time. His *Ignite With Barry Meguiar* radio features are heard daily on over nine hundred Christian radio stations, and his *Ignite With Barry Meguiar* podcasts are heard via Apple Podcasts, Google Podcasts, Spotify, YouTube, Amazon Music, and IgniteAmerica.com.

Visit us:

IgniteAmerica.com

and

SeekingGod.org